casual cooking

Go on, it's healthy

casual cooking

Go on, it's healthy

This edition published by Parragon Books Ltd in 2015
LOVE FOOD is an imprint of Parragon Books Ltd

Parragon Books Ltd
Chartist House
15–17 Trim Street
Bath BA1 1HA, UK
www.parragon.com/lovefood

ISBN 978-1-4723-8487-4

Printed in China

Cover photography by Charlie Richards
Designed by Beth Kalynka
Nutritional analysis by Judith Wills

Notes for the Reader
This book uses both metric and imperial measurements. Follow the same units of measurement throughout; do not mix metric and imperial. All spoon measurements are level: teaspoons are assumed to be 5 ml, and tablespoons are assumed to be 15 ml. Unless otherwise stated, milk is assumed to be full fat, eggs and individual vegetables are medium, and pepper is freshly ground black pepper. Unless otherwise stated, all root vegetables should be peeled prior to using.

Garnishes, decorations and serving suggestions are all optional and not necessarily included in the recipe ingredients or method. Any optional ingredients and seasoning to taste are not included in the nutritional analysis. The times given are an approximate guide only. Preparation times differ according to the techniques used by different people and the cooking times may also vary from those given. Optional ingredients, variations or serving suggestions have not been included in the time calculations. Nutritional values are per serving (Serves...) or per item (Makes...).

While the author has made all reasonable efforts to ensure that the information contained in this book is accurate and up to date at the time of publication, anyone reading this book should note the following important points:-
Medical and pharmaceutical knowledge is constantly changing and the author and the publisher cannot and do not guarantee the accuracy or appropriateness of the contents of this book;
In any event, this book is not intended to be, and should not be relied upon, as a substitute for appropriate, tailored professional advice. Both the author and the publisher strongly recommend that a doctor or other healthcare professional is consulted before embarking on major dietary changes;
For the reasons set out above, and to the fullest extent permitted by law, the author and publisher: (i) cannot and do not accept any legal duty of care or responsibility in relation to the accuracy or appropriateness of the contents of this book, even where expressed as 'advice' or using other words to this effect; and (ii) disclaim any liability, loss, damage or risk that may be claimed or incurred as a consequence – directly or indirectly – of the use and/or application of any of the contents of this book.

contents

symbols

reduced sat fat — Recipes with reduced saturated fat

reduced calorie — Recipes with a low calorie count

reduced sugar — Recipes with reduced sugar

High protein — Recipes that are high in protein

High fibre — Recipes that are high in fibre

see page 26 for more

Breakfast is the most important meal of the day — and it doesn't have to be a boring piece of toast! The recipes in this chapter are designed to give you a nutritious and wholesome start to the day, with dishes including eggs, pancakes and muffins, to granola, porridge and more!

rise & shine!

cranberry & seed muesli

prep: 15 mins, plus soaking
cook: no cooking

175 g/6 oz jumbo porridge oats

40 g/1½ oz rye flakes

40 g/1½ oz whole unblanched almonds, roughly chopped

40 g/1½ oz dried cranberries

2 tbsp sunflower seeds

2 tbsp pumpkin seeds

2 tbsp golden linseeds

2 crisp eating apples

400 ml/14 fl oz apple juice, plus extra to pour (optional)

1. Place the oats, rye flakes, almonds, cranberries, sunflower seeds, pumpkin seeds and linseeds in a large bowl and stir well.

2. Core and roughly grate the apples and stir thoroughly into the dry ingredients.

3. Stir in the apple juice, cover, and leave the muesli to soak for about an hour, or refrigerate overnight.

4. To serve, spoon the mixture into six serving bowls. Serve with a small jug of extra apple juice, if using, for pouring over the muesli.

reduced
sat fat

top tip

Mix a larger batch of the dry
ingredients and store in an airtight
container for 3–4 weeks, ready to
add the fresh apple and juice.

cals: 308   fat: 10.4g   sat fat: 1.2g   fibre: 8g   carbs: 47.7g   sugar: 16.4g   salt: trace   protein: 9.6g

nectarine crunch

prep: 15 mins
cook: no cooking

4 nectarines

2 tbsp peach jam

2 tbsp peach juice

175 g/6 oz raisin and nut crunchy oat cereal

300 g/10½ oz low-fat natural yogurt

1. Cut the nectarines in half, then remove and discard the stones. Chop the flesh into bite-sized pieces and reserve a few slices for decoration.

2. Place the peach jam and juice in a bowl and mix together. Place a few of the nectarine pieces in the bottom of three sundae glasses. Top with half of the oat cereal and a spoonful of the yogurt.

3. Add a few more of the nectarine pieces and spoon over a little of the jam mixture. Repeat the layers with the remaining ingredients, finishing with a spoonful of yogurt. Sprinkle any remaining oat cereal over the top of each sundae. Decorate with the reserved nectarine slices and serve immediately.

variation

Try using ripe plums instead of nectarines for a rich, autumnal twist. Sprinkle over a little cinnamon for a final flourish.

High fibre

cals: 438   fat: 9.9g   sat fat: 3.4g   fibre: 6.8g   carbs: 77.7g   sugar: 48.6g   salt: 0.4g   protein: 11.2g

super seedy granola

prep: 20 mins, plus cooling
cook: 30-35 mins

150 g/5½ oz porridge oats
40 g/1½ oz pumpkin seeds
40 g/1½ oz sunflower seeds
40 g/1½ oz sesame seeds
1 tsp ground cinnamon
2 tbsp light muscovado sugar
2 tbsp olive oil
2 tbsp clear honey
juice of 1 small orange
40 g/1½ oz dried apple slices, diced
40 g/1½ oz dried blueberries
40 g/1½ oz dried cranberries

1. Preheat the oven to 160°C/325°F/Gas Mark 3. Put the oats, pumpkin seeds, sunflower seeds and sesame seeds in an 18 x 28-cm/7 x 11-inch roasting tin. Sprinkle with the cinnamon and sugar, and stir.

2. Drizzle the oil, honey and orange juice over the top and mix together. Bake in the preheated oven for 30–35 minutes, stirring after 15 minutes, to move the mixture in the corners to the centre. Return to the oven and stir every 5–10 minutes, until the granola is golden brown.

3. Scatter the dried apple, blueberries and cranberries over the top and leave the granola to cool and harden. Spoon into a plastic container or spring-clip preserving jar and store in the refrigerator for up to 4 days.

serves 6

variation

Replace the seeds with the same
quantities of your favourite nuts for
a more classic granola.

cals: 361   fat: 16.4g   sat fat: 2.2g   fibre: 6g   carbs: 47.2g   sugar: 22.7   salt: trace   protein: 9g

barley porridge with grilled peaches

85 g/3 oz barley flakes

85 g/3 oz porridge oats

350 ml/12 fl oz cold water

700 ml/1¼ pints unsweetened almond milk

4 tsp maca (powdered superfood)

2 peaches, halved, stoned and sliced

1 papaya, halved, deseeded, peeled and sliced

4 tsp runny honey, plus extra to serve (optional)

½ tsp ground cinnamon

1. Put the barley flakes, porridge oats, water and almond milk in a saucepan. Bring to the boil over a medium–high heat, then reduce the heat to medium and simmer for 5–10 minutes, stirring often, until soft and thickened. Stir in the maca.

2. Preheat the grill to medium–high. Line the rack with foil, then lay the peaches and papaya on top, drizzle with the honey and sprinkle with the cinnamon. Grill for 3–4 minutes, or until just beginning to caramelize.

3. Spoon the porridge into bowls, top with the hot peaches and papaya, and drizzle with a little extra honey, if using.

fact

The beautiful tropical papaya is bursting with vitamin C, potassium and folic acid. It is also said to be good for the skin.

cals: 254   fat: 4.2g   sat fat: 0.6g   fibre: 8.9g   carbs: 48.5g   sugar: 15g   salt: 0.3g   protein: 6.8g

yogurt with orange & toasted seeds

prep: 10 mins, plus cooling
cook: 5 mins

2 tsp linseeds
2 tsp pumpkin seeds
2 tsp chia seeds
200 g/7 oz Greek-style natural yogurt
grated zest of 1 small orange,
  plus 1 tsp juice

top tip

Prepare a larger quantity of the toasted seeds and store in a clean, dry jar. Scatter over porridge, fruit, or even on salads for a healthy boost

1. Place a small frying pan over a medium heat. When it is hot, tip in the seeds. Toast, stirring constantly with a wooden spoon, until they start to turn brown and release a nutty aroma. Tip them onto a plate and leave to cool.

2. Spoon the yogurt into two glass pots or serving bowls, then scatter the seeds on top, followed by the orange zest. Sprinkle over the orange juice and serve immediately.

2

serves 2

reduced sugar

cals: 166   fat: 10g   sat fat: 4.2g   fibre: 3.4g   carbs: 8.4g   sugar: 4.8g   salt: trace   protein: 11.7g

quinoa scrambled eggs

prep: 15 mins
cook: 15-17 mins

5 tbsp water
½ tbsp white quinoa, rinsed
4 large eggs
1½ tbsp snipped fresh chives
40 g/1½ oz butter
salt and pepper
sourdough toast, to serve (optional)

1. Put the water and quinoa into a small saucepan and bring to the boil over a medium heat. Reduce the heat, cover and simmer over a very low heat for 10 minutes, or until most of the liquid has evaporated. Remove from the heat, but leave the pan covered for a further 7 minutes to allow the grains to swell. Fluff up with a fork and set aside.

2. Lightly beat the eggs with the chives, adding salt and pepper to taste.

3. Melt the butter in a heavy-based frying pan over a low heat. Pour in the egg mixture and cook for about 2 minutes, stirring constantly with a wooden spoon, until the eggs are creamy but not yet solid. Gently stir in the quinoa, then pile onto warm sourdough toast, if using, and serve immediately.

High
protein

top tip

The secret to good scrambled eggs
is 'low and slow'. Cook them slowly
over a low heat for the best result

cals: 490   fat: 41.6g   sat fat: 11.8g   fibre: 7g   carbs: 10.2g   sugar: 1.4g   salt: 3.1g   protein: 28.7g

avocado, bacon & chilli frittata

prep: 20 mins
cook: 12-18 mins

1 tbsp vegetable oil

8 streaky bacon rashers, roughly chopped

6 eggs, beaten

3 tbsp double cream

2 large avocados, peeled and sliced

1 red chilli, deseeded and thinly sliced

juice of ½ lime

salt and pepper

1. Preheat the grill to medium. Heat the oil in a 20-cm/8-inch ovenproof frying pan over a medium heat. Add the bacon and fry, stirring, for 4–5 minutes, or until crisp and golden. Using a slotted spoon, transfer the bacon to a plate lined with kitchen paper. Remove the pan from the heat.

2. Pour the eggs into a bowl, add the cream and season with salt and pepper, then beat. Return the pan to the heat. When it is hot, pour in the egg mixture and cook for 1–2 minutes, without stirring. Sprinkle the bacon and avocado on top and cook for a further 2–3 minutes, or until the frittata is almost set and the underside is golden brown.

3. Place the frittata under the grill and cook for 3–4 minutes, or until the top is golden brown and the egg is set. Scatter with the chilli and squeeze over the lime juice. Cut into wedges and serve.

top tip

This frittata works best with really crispy bacon. Cook the bacon over a medium heat to a dark, golden colour, then drain on kitchen paper.

serves 4

cals: 518   fat: 41.6g   sat fat: 11.8g   fibre: 7g   carbs: 10.2g   sugar: 1.4g   salt: 3.1g   protein: 28.7g

courgette rosti with eggs & salmon

prep: 30 mins
cook: 18-26 mins

3 large eggs
1 tbsp double cream
2 tsp finely snipped fresh chives
15 g/½ oz butter
2 large slices of smoked salmon, to serve
salt and pepper

rosti
300 g/10½ oz courgette, grated
2 tsp quinoa flour
20 g/¾ oz Parmesan cheese, grated
1 large egg yolk
1 tbsp double cream
1 tbsp vegetable oil

1. Preheat the oven to 110°C/225°F/ Gas Mark ¼. To make the rosti, lay a clean tea towel on a work surface and pile the courgette in the centre. Holding the tea towel over the sink, gather the sides together and twist them tightly until all the liquid from the courgette has run out.

2. Put the courgette, flour, Parmesan, egg yolk and cream in a bowl and mix well. Roll the mixture into two balls and flatten them with the palms of your hands to make thick patties. Heat the oil in a small frying pan over a medium–low heat. Cook the rostis for 5–8 minutes on each side, or until golden brown. Remove from the heat, transfer to a baking sheet and put them in the oven to keep warm.

3. To make the scrambled eggs, crack the eggs into a bowl, add the cream and chives and season with salt and pepper. Beat with a fork until evenly mixed. Wipe the frying pan clean with kitchen paper, then melt the butter in the pan over a low heat. Pour in the egg mixture and cook, stirring, for 5–6 minutes, or until the eggs are just set.

4. Put the warm rostis on two plates. Spoon over the scrambled eggs, then top with the salmon and a little black pepper to serve.

cals: 538   fat: 41.6g   sat fat: 16g   fibre: 2.1g   carbs: 10.1g   sugar: 4.5g   salt: 4.5g   protein: 31.2g

breakfast burrito

prep: 15–20 mins
cook: 8–10 mins

2 egg whites
pinch of salt
¼ tsp pepper
1 spring onion, thinly sliced
vegetable oil spray
30 g/1 oz red or green pepper, diced
2 tbsp canned black beans, rinsed
1 wholemeal flour tortilla, warmed
15 g/½ oz crumbled feta cheese
2 tbsp fresh salsa
1 tsp finely chopped coriander,
  plus extra to garnish

1. In a small bowl, combine the egg whites, salt, pepper and spring onion, and stir well.

2. Spray a non-stick frying pan with vegetable oil spray and place it over a medium–high heat. Add the red pepper and cook, stirring, for about 3 minutes or until it begins to soften. Reduce the heat to medium, pour in the egg mixture and cook, stirring often, for a further 1–2 minutes, or until the egg sets.

3. Put the beans in a microwave-safe bowl and microwave on high for about 1 minute, or until heated through.

4. Spoon the cooked egg mixture onto the tortilla. Top with the beans, cheese, salsa and coriander. Serve immediately, garnished with whole coriander leaves.

reduced
sat fat

top tip

To warm the tortilla, heat a dry frying pan over a medium heat and place inside. Heat until just warm.

cals: 278   fat: 8.1g   sat fat: 3.3g   fibre: 7.4g   carbs: 31.2g   sugar: 8.4g   salt: 1.5g   protein: 16g

nutritional symbols

 reduced sat fat Recipes with this symbol fall within the 10% of daily calories allowed for saturated fat.

 reduced calorie Recipes with this symbol are suitable for those on a typical weight-maintenance diet.

 reduced sugar Recipes with this symbol fall under the recommended daily allowance for sugar.

 High protein This symbol indicates that a recipe contains at least 15% of its total calories in protein.

 High fibre Recipes with this symbol contain between 3–7g fibre per serving, depending on the type of dish.

watch out for these!

Reduced sat fat — Recipes containing the 'reduced sat fat' symbol are perfect for those who are watching their weight. One way to reduce the total amount of saturated fat in your diet is to try some different cooking methods, such as poaching or steaming, rather than frying food in cooking oils.

Reduced calorie — Recipes with the 'reduced calorie' symbol are also ideal for those on a weight loss plan. In order to lose weight you must consume fewer calories than you burn to create what is called a 'calorie deficit'. You can do this by eating a little less and/or exercising more, as well as selecting lower-calorie foods.

Reduced sugar — Sugar, whether refined or natural, is in almost everything we eat, and has been targeted by health specialists for its link to obesity, diabetes and cardiovascular disease. The best way to cut down your sugar intake is to eat natural, whole and unprocessed foods where possible.

High protein — Protein, rather than refined carbohydrates such as white bread and pasta, is an excellent source of energy and can leave you feeling fuller, longer. Lean, unprocessed sources of protein such as chicken and turkey breast are easy to cook and can be used in a variety of dishes.

High fibre — Recipes with the 'high fibre' symbol contain useful sources of soluble fibre, such as fruit, vegetables and whole grains. A diet rich in fibre has many health benefits and can assist with the prevention of certain diseases as well as improving overall digestive health.

buckwheat pancakes with ricotta

prep: 30 mins
cook: 30 mins

3 eggs, separated
225 ml/8 fl oz buttermilk
1 tbsp melted butter, cooled slightly
75 g/2¾ oz buckwheat flour
55 g/2 oz plain flour
2 tsp baking powder
1 tsp caster sugar
¼ tsp salt
vegetable oil, for brushing

ricotta topping
225 g/8 oz ricotta cheese
1 tsp caster sugar
finely grated rind of 1 orange
1 piece stem ginger, finely chopped,
   plus syrup from the jar to serve
   (optional)

1. To make the topping, combine all the ingredients in a bowl, then set aside. Whisk together the egg yolks, buttermilk and melted butter until well blended.

2. Combine the flours, baking powder, sugar and salt in a large bowl. Make a well in the centre and pour in the egg yolk mixture. Mix together with a fork, drawing in the dry ingredients until a smooth batter forms.

3. Whisk the egg whites in a large bowl until they hold stiff peaks. Using a metal spoon, fold one third of the egg white into the batter to loosen it, then fold in the remaining egg.

4. Lightly brush a heavy-based frying pan with oil and place over a medium heat. Spoon in 4 tablespoons of the batter, spreading it into an 8–9-cm/3¼–3½-inch circle with the back of a metal spoon. Cook for 1½–2 minutes, or until bubbles appear on the surface. Turn and cook on the other side for 1½ minutes. Set aside and keep warm while you cook the remaining batter.

5. Spread the pancakes with the topping, drizzle over a little ginger syrup, if using, and serve immediately.

makes 8

cals: 189   fat: 9.8g   sat fat: 4.5g   fibre: 1.2g   carbs: 16.2g   sugar: 3.7g   salt: 0.8g   protein: 8.9g

wholemeal crêpes

prep: 25 mins
cook: 25 mins

mushroom filling

1 tbsp olive oil

1 garlic clove, finely chopped

1 shallot, finely chopped

675 g/1 lb 8 oz button mushrooms, sliced

½ tsp salt

½ tsp pepper

crêpes

150 g/5½ oz wholemeal flour

2 large eggs

300 ml/10 fl oz skimmed milk

¼ tsp salt

2 tbsp unsalted butter, melted

vegetable oil spray

115 g/4 oz reduced-fat soured cream,
  to serve

3 tbsp finely chopped chives,
  to garnish

1. To make the mushroom filling, heat the oil in a large frying pan over a medium–high heat. Add the garlic and shallot and cook for about 5 minutes, stirring occasionally, until soft. Add the mushrooms and continue to cook for about 5 minutes, stirring, until they soften. Season to taste with the salt and pepper. Remove from heat and set aside. To make the crêpes, place the flour, eggs, milk, salt and butter in a medium bowl. Beat together with an electric hand-held mixer.

2. Coat a large, non-stick frying pan with vegetable oil spray and place it over a medium heat. When the frying pan is hot, ladle the crêpe mixture, about 60 ml/2 fl oz at a time, into the hot frying pan. Tilt the frying pan in a circular motion to spread the mixture into a thin, even round about 15 cm/6 inches in diameter. Cook for about 1 minute, until the crêpe begins to colour lightly underneath. Gently flip the crêpe over and cook for a further 45 seconds on the other side. Keep the crêpe warm in a low oven while you cook the rest of the mixture.

3. When all of the crêpes are cooked, spoon 2–3 tablespoons of the mushroom filling onto each crêpe and fold in half twice. Serve with a dollop of soured cream and garnish with finely chopped chives.

reduced calorie

cals: 239   fat: 11.2g   sat fat: 4.5g   fibre: 3.9g   carbs: 24.6g   sugar: 5.9g   salt: 0.9g   protein: 12.1g

blueberry & oat breakfast bars

prep: 20–25 mins, plus cooling
cook: 20–25 mins

115 g/4 oz unsalted butter

100 g/3½ oz quinoa flour

100 g/3½ oz rolled oats

pinch of salt

½ tsp freshly grated nutmeg

1 tsp ground cinnamon

½ tsp ground allspice

½ tsp baking powder

½ tsp bicarbonate of soda

2 tbsp rice malt syrup or honey

1 large egg, beaten

60 g/2¼ oz blueberries

30 g/1 oz cranberries, roughly chopped (optional)

1. Preheat the oven to 160°C/325°F/Gas Mark 3. Line a 26 x 16-cm/10½ x 6¼-inch rectangular cake tin with baking paper. Melt the butter in a small saucepan, then pour it into a large bowl. Add all the remaining ingredients apart from the blueberries and cranberries to the bowl and mix to a chunky batter. Carefully stir in the blueberries and cranberries, if using.

2. Pour the mixture into the prepared tin and spread it into an even layer using the back of a spoon. Bake for 20–25 minutes, or until golden brown and set. Transfer to a wire rack to cool. After 10 minutes, cut into 12 bars, then leave to cool completely.

fact

Blueberries are high in antioxidants and vitamin C, and they're easy to add to any breakfast dish for an immediate health and flavour boost

reduced sugar

cals: 156   fat: 9.6g   sat fat: 5.3g   fibre: 1.4g   carbs: 14.7g   sugar: 3.5g   salt: 0.4g   protein: 3.2g

mini coffee & pecan muffins

prep: 20–25 mins, plus cooling
cook: 20 mins

50 g/1¾ oz coconut flour

¼ tsp baking powder

½ tsp bicarbonate of soda

1 tbsp artifical sweetener,
  such as stevia

30 g/1 oz pecan nuts, roughly chopped

150 ml/5 fl oz soured cream

5 tbsp vegetable oil

2 large eggs, beaten

5 tbsp prepared espresso or strong
  instant coffee

1 tsp rice malt syrup or honey

salt

fact

Rice malt syrup is made from fermented cooked rice. It's a blend of carbohydrates, maltose and glucose, and releases energy much slower than its sugary counterparts, such as golden syrup.

1. Preheat the oven to 160°C/325°F/ Gas Mark 3. Put nine mini muffin cases into a mini muffin tray or use squares of baking paper.

2. Put the flour, baking powder, bicarbonate of soda, artificial sweetener, 20 g/¾ oz pecan nuts and a small pinch of salt in a large bowl, and mix well. Add the soured cream, oil, eggs and 4 tablespoons of espresso, and stir until evenly mixed. Leave to stand for a moment, then spoon the mixture into the mini muffin cases.

3. Bake for 20 minutes, or until well risen and the tops spring back when pressed with a fingertip. Leave to cool for 5 minutes, then transfer to a wire rack.

4. To make the topping, put the rice malt syrup and remaining 1 tablespoon of espresso in a bowl and mix. Spoon a small drizzle over each muffin. Sprinkle on the remaining 10 g/¼ oz pecan nuts and serve warm, or store in an airtight container for up to two days.

makes 9

reduced
sat fat

cals: 167   fat: 15.1g   sat fat: 4.1g   fibre: 2.3g   carbs: 4.9g   sugar: 1.7g   salt: 0.6g   protein: 3.3g

banana, goji & hazelnut bread

prep: 25 mins, plus cooling
cook: 50-60 mins

85 g/3 oz butter, softened, plus extra to grease

115 g/4 oz light muscovado sugar

2 eggs

3 bananas (500 g/1 lb 2 oz with the skins on), peeled and mashed

115 g/4 oz wholemeal plain flour

115 g/4 oz plain flour

2 tsp baking powder

55 g/2 oz unblanched hazelnuts, roughly chopped

40 g/1½ oz goji berries

40 g/1½ oz dried banana chips

1. Preheat the oven to 180°C/350°F/Gas Mark 4. Grease a 900-g/2-lb loaf tin and line the base and two long sides with baking paper.

2. Cream the butter and sugar together in a large bowl. Beat in the eggs, one at a time, then the banana.

3. Put the flours and baking powder in a bowl and mix well. Add to the banana mixture and beat until smooth. Add the hazelnuts and goji berries and stir well.

4. Spoon the mixture into the prepared tin, smooth the top flat then sprinkle with the banana chips. Bake for 50–60 minutes, or until the loaf is well risen, has cracked slightly and a skewer comes out clean when inserted into the centre.

5. Leave to cool for 5 minutes, then loosen the edges with a round-bladed knife and turn out onto a wire rack. Leave to cool completely, then peel away the paper. Store in an airtight tin for up to three days.

top tip

Goji berries have long been hailed as a superfood and they can easily be found in health food stores, some supermarkets and online.

reduced calorie

cals: 299   fat: 12.1g   sat fat: 5.1g   fibre: 4g   carbs: 44.3g   sugar: 18.6g   salt: 0.5g   protein: 6.1g

mixed berry smoothie

reduced calorie

prep: 20 mins, plus soaking
cook: no cooking

1 tbsp chia seeds (preferably white)

375 ml/13 fl oz soya milk

125 g/4½ oz frozen mixed berries,
   slightly thawed, plus extra to
   decorate (optional)

1 ripe banana, sliced

3 ready-to-eat dried apricots,
   roughly chopped

2 tbsp honey

lemon juice, to taste

fact

Packed with sustaining protein and
healthy fats, chia seeds are easy
to add to a variety of meals and they add
body and texture to any smoothie.

1. Put the chia seeds into a small bowl.
Stir in 125 ml/4 fl oz of the soya milk and
leave to soak for 15 minutes, whisking
every 5 minutes to prevent the seeds from
clumping together.

2. Put the remaining ingredients into a
blender. Add the soaked chia seeds and their
gel-like liquid. Process for 1 minute, or until
smooth. Pour into glasses and decorate with a
few berries, if using.

cals: 133   fat: 2.4g   sat fat: 0.3g   fibre: 3.5g   carbs: 24.8g   sugar: 19.1g   salt: 0.1g   protein: 4g

ruby fruit reviver

prep: 15 mins
cook: no cooking

1 ruby red grapefruit, zest and a little
   pith removed, deseeded and roughly
   chopped
¼ cucumber, roughly chopped
150 g/5½ oz strawberries, hulled
small handful of crushed ice (optional)

1. Put the grapefruit and cucumber in a
blender and process until smooth. Add the
strawberries and crushed ice, if using, and
process until blended. Pour into a glass and
serve immediately.

top tip

Morning smoothies are great for
injecting extra superfoods into the diet. Try
adding a tablespoon of maca powder or chia
seeds before blending.

lychee & pineapple pep-up

High fibre

prep: 20 mins, plus standing
cook: no cooking

1½ lemon grass stems

4 tbsp boiling water

6 lychees, peeled and stoned

½ small pineapple, peeled and cut into thick slices

¼ honeydew melon, thickly sliced and peel removed

small handful of ice (optional)

1. Cut the whole lemon grass stem in half lengthways, then crossways. Bruise it with a rolling pin to release its flavour, then put it in a shallow bowl and add the boiling water. Cover and leave to go cold, then drain and reserve the soaking water.

2. Feed the softened lemon grass, lychees and pineapple, then melon through a juicer. Mix in the reserved soaking water. Half-fill a glass with ice, if using, then pour in the juice and serve immediately with the remaining half-lemon grass stem as a stirrer.

fact

Lychees originated in China and can be found in Asian grocers and some supermarkets. They have a similar texture to grapes with fragrant flesh.

cals: 280   fat: 0.6g   sat fat: 0.2g   fibre: 7g   carbs: 70.7g   sugar: 57.9g   salt: 0.1g   protein: 3.7g

super sides

There isn't anything nicer than sharing food, but often sides and small dishes added to a main meal can be full of empty calories and carbohydrates. This chapter shows you how easy it is to ring the changes with lots of fresh, healthy and vitamin-rich small dishes for sharing or eating as sides.

sides, smalls & sharers

quinoa salad with
fennel & orange

prep: 25-30 mins, plus cooling
cook: 15-17 mins

850 ml/1½ pints vegetable stock

225 g/8 oz quinoa, rinsed and drained

3 oranges

250 g/9 oz fennel bulbs, thinly sliced using a mandolin, green feathery tops reserved and torn into small pieces

2 spring onions, finely chopped

15 g/½ oz fresh flat-leaf parsley, roughly chopped

dressing

juice of ½ lemon

3 tbsp olive oil

pepper

fact

Quinoa is native to Peru and Bolivia and is said to be the only plant food that contains all essential amino acids, putting it on a par with animal protein.

1. Bring the stock to the boil in a saucepan, add the quinoa and simmer for 10–12 minutes, or until the germs separate from the seeds. Drain off the stock and discard, then spoon the quinoa into a salad bowl and leave to cool.

2. Grate the rind from two of the oranges and put it in a jam jar. Cut a slice off the top and bottom of each of the three oranges, then remove the peel in thin vertical slices and discard. Cut between the membranes to remove the orange segments, then squeeze the juice from the membranes into the jar. Add the orange segments, fennel slices, spring onions and parsley to the quinoa.

3. To make the dressing, add the lemon juice and oil to the jam jar, season to taste with pepper, screw on the lid and shake well. Drizzle over the salad and toss together. Garnish with the fennel tops and serve immediately.

cals: 368   fat: 15.3g   sat fat: 2.8g   fibre: 7g   carbs: 51.1g   sugar: 8.1g   salt: 2.2g   protein: 9.8g

indian spiced slaw

prep: 20 mins, plus cooling
cook: 5 mins

150 g/5½ oz low-fat natural yogurt
175 g/6 oz red cabbage, shredded
40 g/1½ oz kale, shredded
1 red apple, cored and coarsely grated
1 large carrot, coarsely grated
salt and pepper

topping
2 tbsp pumpkin seeds
2 tbsp sunflower seeds
2 tbsp flaked almonds
1½ tsp garam masala
½ tsp turmeric
1 tbsp sunflower oil

1. To make the topping, preheat a frying pan over a medium heat. Put the pumpkin seeds, sunflower seeds, almonds, ½ teaspoon of garam masala and ¼ teaspoon of turmeric in the hot pan and pour on the oil. Cook for 3–4 minutes, stirring often, until the almonds are golden brown. Leave to cool.

2. To make the dressing, put the yogurt and remaining 1 teaspoon of garam masala and ¼ teaspoon of turmeric in a large bowl, then season to taste with salt and pepper, and stir well.

3. Add the cabbage, kale, apple and carrot to the bowl and toss gently together. Divide the salad between four bowls, sprinkle on the topping and serve.

fact

Red cabbage, kale and carrots are all high in antioxidants, and the vitamin C-rich apples will help boost your immune system.

High
fibre

cals: 193   fat: 11.9g   sat fat: 1.6g   fibre: 4.6g   carbs: 17.6g   sugar: 9.8g   salt: 1.6g   protein: 7g

super green salad

2 tbsp pumpkin seeds

2 tbsp sunflower seeds

2 tbsp sesame seeds

4 tsp tamari or soy sauce

250 g/9 oz broccoli, cut into florets

85 g/3 oz baby spinach

55 g/2 oz kale, thinly shredded

15 g/½ oz fresh coriander,
    roughly chopped

2 avocados, stoned, peeled and sliced

juice of 2 limes

dressing

3 tbsp flaxseed oil

2 tsp runny honey

pepper

fact

This mix of greens means lots of chlorophyll (the pigment that makes the green colour), which increases haemoglobin in the blood, making it more oxygen-rich and healthy.

1. Place a frying pan over a high heat. Add the pumpkin, sunflower and sesame seeds, cover and dry-fry for 3–4 minutes, or until lightly toasted and beginning to pop, shaking the pan from time to time. Remove from the heat and stir in the tamari.

2. Half-fill the base of a steamer with water, bring to the boil, then put the broccoli in the steamer top, cover with a lid and steam for 3–5 minutes, or until tender. Transfer to a salad bowl and add the spinach, kale and coriander. Put the avocados and half the lime juice in a small bowl and toss well, then tip them into the salad bowl.

3. To make the dressing, put the remaining lime juice, the oil, honey and a little pepper in a small jug and fork together. Sprinkle the toasted seeds over the salad and serve immediately with the dressing.

serves 4

reduced sugar

cals: 387 fat: 33g sat fat: 3.9g fibre: 10.7g carbs: 22.8g sugar: 5g salt: 0.8g protein: 8.7g

chicken, papaya & avocado salad

prep: 25 mins
cook: 8-10 mins

2 skinless, boneless chicken breasts, weighing about 150 g/5½ oz each

2 tbsp olive oil

100 g/3½ oz peppery green salad leaves, such as rocket, mizuna, curly endive and watercress

1 large papaya, peeled, deseeded and thickly sliced

1 ripe avocado, peeled, stoned and thickly sliced

25 g/1 oz toasted hazelnuts, halved

2 tbsp red or white quinoa sprouts

salt and pepper

dressing

2 tbsp lime juice

6 tbsp hazelnut oil

salt and pepper

1. Place the chicken breasts on a board. With the knife parallel to the board, slice each breast in half horizontally to make four fillets in total. Place the fillets between two sheets of clingfilm and pound with a rolling pin to a thickness of about 8 mm/⅜ inch.

2. Heat the oil in a large frying pan. Add the chicken and fry over a medium–high heat for 3–4 minutes on each side, until golden on the outside and no longer pink in the middle. Transfer to a warmed plate and season to taste with salt and pepper. Slice the chicken lengthways into 2 cm/⅜ inch wide strips.

3. Divide the salad leaves between two plates. Arrange the chicken, papaya and avocado on top. Sprinkle with the toasted hazelnuts and quinoa sprouts.

4. To make the dressing, whisk together all the ingredients until smooth and creamy. Pour over the salad and serve immediately.

High protein

cals: 1008   fat: 82g   sat fat: 8.5g   fibre: 12.7g   carbs: 35.3g   sugar: 14.3g   salt: 2g   protein: 38.9g

vietnamese shredded chicken salad

prep: 30 mins, plus cooling
cook: 1 hour 40 mins-1 hour 55 mins

1 chicken, weighing 1 kg/2 lb 4 oz

2 lemon grass stems, halved lengthways

1 celery stick, sliced

1 onion, quartered

2 carrots, sliced

1.2 litres/2 pints cold water

2 tbsp soy sauce

salad

2 carrots

1 courgette

150 g/5½ oz ready-to-eat beansprouts

2 Little Gem lettuces, thickly sliced

25 g/1 oz fresh coriander,
  roughly chopped

dressing

finely grated rind and juice of ½ lime

1 red chilli, deseeded and finely chopped

2 tsp fish sauce

1. To cook the chicken, put it, breast-side down, in a deep saucepan only a little bigger than the bird. Add the lemon grass, celery, onion and carrots. Pour in the water, ensuring it covers the bird, and add the soy sauce. Bring to the boil, cover and simmer for 1 hour, or until cooked through. Lift the chicken out of the pan. To check it is cooked, pierce the thickest part of the leg between the drumstick and thigh with a skewer; any juices should be piping hot and clear, with no traces of pink. Cover and leave to cool. Boil the stock for 30–45 minutes, until reduced to 250 ml/9 fl oz. Strain through a sieve and leave to cool.

2. Shave the carrots and courgette into long, thin ribbons using a swivel-bladed vegetable peeler, and put them in a salad bowl. Add the beansprouts, lettuce and coriander, and toss.

3. To make the dressing, strain the fat off the chicken stock, then measure out 150 ml/5 fl oz of the liquid and pour it into a large bowl. Add the lime rind and juice, chilli and fish sauce and mix. Take the meat off the chicken, shred it into thin strips (discarding the skin and bones) and add it to the dressing, then toss gently together. Spoon the salad onto four plates, top with the chicken and dressing, and serve.

High protein

serves 4

cals: 332   fat: 11.8g   sat fat: 3g   fibre: 4.3g   carbs: 10.2g   sugar: 4.8g   salt: 1.1g   protein: 44.6g

rainbow nori rolls

prep: 30-35 mins, plus chilling
cook: 27-30 mins

175 g/6 oz sushi rice

700 ml/1¼ pints cold water

2 tbsp mirin

1 tbsp light olive oil

100 g/3½ oz asparagus tips

4 sheets nori

105 g/3¾ oz sliced sushi ginger, drained

25 g/1 oz kale, cut into thin strips

1 small red pepper, halved, deseeded and cut into thin strips

1 small yellow pepper, halved, deseeded and cut into thin strips

100 g/3½ oz carrots, cut into matchstick strips

100 g/3½ oz cooked beetroot in natural juices, drained and cut into matchstick strips

2 tbsp tamari

2 tbsp Chinese rice wine

salt

1. Put the rice and water into a saucepan with a little salt and bring to the boil, stirring occasionally. Reduce the heat and gently simmer for 18–20 minutes, until the rice is soft and has absorbed all the water. Stir occasionally towards the end of cooking so that the rice doesn't stick to the base of the pan. Remove from the heat and stir in the mirin. Leave to cool for 10 minutes.

2. Heat the oil in a frying pan, add the asparagus and fry over a medium heat for 3–4 minutes until just soft, then set aside.

3. Separate the nori sheets and place one on a piece of clingfilm set on top of a bamboo sushi mat. Thinly spread one quarter of the warm rice over the top to cover the nori sheet completely.

4. Arrange one quarter of the ginger in an overlapping line a little up from one edge of the nori. Arrange one quarter of the asparagus and kale next to it, then one quarter of the red pepper and yellow pepper, then one quarter of the carrot and beetroot, leaving a border of rice about 2 cm/¾ inch wide.

5. Using the clingfilm and the sushi mat, tightly roll the nori around the vegetables, starting from the line of ginger and finishing at the border of rice, which will act as a sticky glue

to seal the roll. Remove the bamboo mat, then twist the ends of the clingfilm to set the shape and place the roll on a tray or small baking sheet. Repeat to make three more nori rolls. Place on the tray and chill for 1 hour, or longer if preferred.

6. To serve, mix the tamari and rice wine together, then spoon into four small dipping bowls set on serving plates. Unwrap each nori roll and cut into five thick slices. Arrange them, cut-side up, on the serving plates and serve immediately.

High
fibre
serves 4

cals: 232   fat: 4.1g   sat fat: 0.7g   fibre: 5.2g   carbs: 42.6g   sugar: 10.7g   salt: 4.3g   protein: 6.4g

beetroot falafel
with pittas

prep: 30-35 mins, plus rising
cook: 35-45 mins

little wholemeal plain flour, to dust

1 quantity kneaded and risen pizza base dough made with 1 tsp roughly crushed cumin seeds added with the yeast

2 x 400 g/14 oz cans of chickpeas in water, drained

1 red onion, finely chopped

2 garlic cloves, thinly sliced

1 tsp cumin seeds, roughly crushed

1 tsp sumac seeds

1 tsp baking powder

2 raw beetroot (approx 175 g/6 oz), coarsely grated

3 tbsp virgin olive oil, to brush

salt and pepper

lettuce leaves, shredded, to serve (optional)

tzatziki

½ cucumber, halved, deseeded and finely chopped

150 g/5½ oz natural yogurt

2 tbsp finely chopped fresh mint

1. Preheat the oven to 220°C/425°F/Gas Mark 7. To make the pittas, lightly dust a work surface with flour. Knead the dough, then cut into four pieces and roll out each piece into an oval. Leave to rise for 10 minutes.

2. Lightly flour two baking sheets, then put them in the oven for 5 minutes. Add the breads to the hot baking sheets and bake for 5–10 minutes, or until lightly browned. Wrap in a clean tea towel to keep them soft.

3. Meanwhile, put the chickpeas in a food processor and process, in small batches, to a coarse paste. Tip into a bowl. Add the onion, garlic, cumin, sumac, baking powder and beetroot. Season with salt and pepper, then mix.

4. Roll the mixture into 20 balls. Brush a large roasting tin with a little oil, then put it in the oven for 5 minutes. Add the falafel and brush generously with more oil. Roast the falafel for 20–25 minutes, turning, until browned and cooked through.

5. Meanwhile, to make the tzatziki, put the cucumber, yogurt and mint in a bowl, season with salt and pepper, and mix well. To serve, split the warm pittas open, spoon in the shredded lettuce, if using, tzatziki and falafel, and serve.

serves 4

reduced sat fat

cals: 483   fat: 14.7g   sat fat: 2.6g   fibre: 7.5g   carbs: 69.1g   sugar: 7.5g   salt: 2.8g   protein: 17.6g

yam, swede & mushroom hash

prep: 20–25 mins
cook: 25–30 mins

3 tbsp olive oil
500 g/1 lb 2 oz yams, diced
280 g/10 oz swedes, diced
1 onion, chopped
175 g/6 oz streaky bacon, sliced, or lardons
250 g/9 oz mushrooms, sliced
4 eggs
salt and pepper
chopped fresh parsley, to garnish

1. Heat the oil in a large, lidded frying pan over a high heat. Add the yams and swedes, stir in the oil to coat and season to taste with salt and pepper. Cook, stirring occasionally, for 10–15 minutes, or until the vegetables are just turning golden.

2. Add the onion and bacon, stir well and continue to cook for 5 minutes, until the onion is soft and the bacon is cooked. Stir in the mushrooms, cover and cook for a further 5 minutes.

3. Make four indentations in the mixture and carefully break an egg into each one. Cover the pan and cook for a further 3–4 minutes, or until the egg whites are firm but the yolks are still soft. Garnish with parsley and serve.

High
protein

top tip

The yam is a very versatile vegetable — it can be roasted, fried, grilled, boiled and, when grated, it can be used in desserts too!

cals: 518   fat: 26.4g   sat fat: 7.2g   fibre: 7.7g   carbs: 45.3g   sugar: 7g   salt: 3.5g   protein: 24.5g

root vegetable fries

900 g/2 lb any combination of
  parsnips, swedes, turnips and carrots,
  cut into 5-mm/¼-inch strips
2 tbsp vegetable oil
1 tsp salt

1. Preheat the oven to 230°C/450°F/
Gas Mark 8. Toss the cut vegetables with the
oil and salt. Spread the vegetables in a single
layer on a large baking sheet and bake in the
preheated oven for about 20 minutes, flipping
them halfway through cooking,
until they are golden brown and cooked.
Remove from the oven and preheat the
grill to medium.

2. Place under the preheated grill for
2–3 minutes, until they begin to crisp up.
Flip them over and return them to the
grill for a further 2 minutes to crisp the
other side. Serve immediately, sprinkled
with salt.

top tip

Try adding a little crushed garlic and a
sprinkling of smoked paprika to the fries before
baking for a tasty, smoky hit

serves 4

reduced calorie

cals: 171   fat: 7.4g   sat fat: 0.8g   fibre: 7.3g   carbs: 25.1g   sugar: 10.8g   salt: 3.2g   protein: 2.1g

what is a healthy diet?

The key to a healthy diet is variety, so try to eat a wide range of food. Dishes offering low nutritional value, such as sugar- and fat-laden cakes and biscuits, can harm you if eaten in large quantities or over a long period of time, as they have been linked to obesity, diabetes, high cholesterol and heart problems, and even cancer. There is nothing wrong with the odd treat, but keep a burger and chips or a gooey slice of chocolate cake as just that, an occasional treat.

In Western countries, 21st-century diseases are more commonly caused by a dietary excess and imbalance than by a nutritional deficiency. It is important to eat foods from all the main food groups: carbohydrates, proteins, fats, vitamins and minerals. Opt for wholegrain foods where possible, as these take a long time to digest, leaving you feeling fuller for longer.

try these top tips...

Drink plenty of water – drinking plenty of water flushes harmful toxins from your system as well as keeping you well hydrated

Get enough sleep – getting plenty of sleep (around 8 hours per night) is essential to overall health and helps with everything from muscle recovery to good brain function

Eat the rainbow – varying the fruit and vegetables you eat means you will always be getting a good range of vitamins and minerals

Cook your own food – not only is cooking an important life skill, but making your own food means you know exactly what has gone into it

Avoid sugar where possible – sugar, whether processed or natural, is in almost everything we eat and eating too much of it can cause a variety of health problems. Try to reduce your intake, or even eliminate it completely from your diet

Grill meat and fish rather than frying – grilling your meat or fish means you can cut down on the amount of fat you use to cook it in. Steaming is another healthy cooking method that requires no fat

Choose clean and lean sources of protein – when choosing protein, opt for mostly lean cuts of meat and fish like turkey and chicken breast, or cod and hake. Fat from animal protein, such as bacon rind, is however a useful source of healthy dietary fat if consumed in moderation

Steer clear of anything white – refined and processed white carbohydrates such as white flour, pasta, bread and rice are quickly absorbed by the body as sugar and can wreak havoc with your health

Reduce your salt intake – salt can creep into many foods we eat, particularly pre-prepared and fast foods, so try to avoid these obvious sources and limit the amount of salt you use in your cooking

spicy chicken with fennel & chilli slaw

prep: 25 mins, plus chilling
cook: 34-42 mins

200 ml/7 fl oz soured cream

½ tsp cayenne pepper

1 garlic clove, crushed

4 chicken thighs and 4 chicken drumsticks (about 850 g/1 lb 14 oz)

2 tsp coarse polenta

2 tbsp quinoa flour

2 tbsp wholemeal plain flour

vegetable oil, for deep-frying

salt and pepper

slaw

200 g/7 oz red cabbage, shredded

400 g/14 oz fennel, shredded

1 red chilli, deseeded and thinly sliced lengthways

100 g/3½ oz Greek-style natural yogurt

juice of ¼ lemon

salt and pepper

1. Put the soured cream, cayenne and garlic in a large bowl and season well with salt and pepper. Add the chicken and toss well. Cover and chill in the refrigerator for 2–3 hours.

2. To make the coleslaw, combine all the ingredients in a large bowl, then season with salt and pepper. Cover with clingfilm and chill in the refrigerator.

3. Mix together the polenta and flours on a plate and season with salt and pepper. Half-fill a heavy-based frying pan with oil and place over a medium-high heat. Heat the oil to 180°C/350°F, or until a cube of bread browns in 30 seconds. Sprinkle the flour mixture over the chicken.

4. Cook the chicken in two batches. Carefully place half the chicken in the oil. Cook for 6–8 minutes, then turn and cook for a further 6–8 minutes, until the coating is a golden brown, the chicken is cooked through to the bone, and the juices run clear when a skewer is inserted into the thickest part of the meat.

5. Transfer the cooked chicken to kitchen paper to drain, then keep warm in a low oven while you cook the second batch. Serve on a sharing board with the coleslaw.

High
protein

cals: 663   fat: 45.5g   sat fat: 13.8g   fibre: 5.2g   carbs: 25.8g   sugar: 6.7g   salt: 2g   protein: 38.1g

chicken satay skewers

prep: 25–30 mins, plus marinating
cook: 6–8 mins

4 skinless, boneless chicken breasts, about 115 g/4 oz each, cut into 2-cm/¾-inch cubes

4 tbsp soy sauce

1 tbsp cornflour

2 garlic cloves, finely chopped

2.5-cm/1-inch piece fresh ginger, peeled and finely chopped

1 cucumber, diced, to serve

peanut sauce

2 tbsp groundnut or vegetable oil

½ onion, finely chopped

1 garlic clove, finely chopped

4 tbsp crunchy peanut butter

4–5 tbsp water

½ tsp chilli powder

1. Put the chicken cubes in a shallow dish. Mix the soy sauce, cornflour, garlic and ginger together in a small bowl and pour over the chicken. Cover and leave to marinate in the refrigerator for at least 2 hours.

2. Meanwhile, soak 12 wooden skewers in cold water for at least 30 minutes. Preheat the grill and thread the chicken pieces onto the wooden skewers. Transfer the skewers to a grill pan and cook under a preheated grill for 3–4 minutes. Turn the skewers over and cook for a further 3–4 minutes, or until cooked through. To make sure the chicken is cooked through, cut into the middle to check that there are no remaining traces of pink or red.

3. Meanwhile, to make the sauce, heat the oil in a saucepan, add the onion and garlic and cook, over a medium heat, stirring frequently, for 3–4 minutes, until softened. Add the peanut butter, water and chilli powder and simmer, for 2–3 minutes, until softened and thinned. Serve the skewers immediately with the warm sauce and diced cucumber.

reduced
sat fat

cals: 339   fat: 18g   sat fat: 3.1g   fibre: 2.5g   carbs: 14.6g   sugar: 4.2g   salt: 2.8g   protein: 31g

turkey goujons with kale & apple slaw

prep: 35 mins, plus chilling
cook: 15 mins

70 g/2½ oz linseeds

40 g/1½ oz sesame seeds

2 eggs

450 g/1 lb skinless and boneless
  turkey breast, thinly sliced

3 tbsp virgin olive oil

salt and pepper

kale & apple slaw

115 g/4 oz red cabbage,
  thinly shredded

25 g/1 oz kale, thinly shredded

1 carrot, coarsely grated

1 dessert apple, cored and
  coarsely grated

1 tsp caraway seeds

60 g/2¼ oz Greek-style natural yogurt

salt and pepper

top tip

An easy way of reducing the
amount of oil in your cooking is to
use an olive oil pump spray instead.

1. Preheat the oven to 220°C/425°F/Gas Mark 7 and put a large baking sheet inside.

2. To make the slaw, put the red cabbage, kale and carrot in a bowl and mix well. Add the apple, caraway seeds and yogurt, season with salt and pepper, and mix well. Cover and chill in the refrigerator until needed.

3. Put the linseeds in a spice mill or blender and process until roughly chopped. Add the sesame seeds and process for a few seconds. Tip the mixture out onto a plate.

4. Crack the eggs into a shallow dish, season with salt and pepper, and beat lightly. Dip each turkey slice into the eggs, then lift it out with a fork and dip both sides into the seed mixture to coat. Brush the hot baking sheet with a little oil, add the turkey slices in a single layer, then drizzle with a little extra olive oil.

5. Bake the turkey, turning the slices once, for 15 minutes, or until golden brown and cooked through. To make sure the turkey is cooked through, cut into the middle and check that there are no remaining traces of pink or red. Serve the goujons with the slaw.

serves 4

High
protein

cals: 463   fat: 26.9g   sat fat: 4.4g   fibre: 8.4g   carbs: 18.8g   sugar: 7.1g   salt: 1.8g   protein: 38.5g

moroccan meatballs

High protein

prep: 35 mins
cook: 15 mins

olive oil spray
450 g/1 lb fresh lamb mince
½ small onion, finely chopped
1 garlic clove, finely chopped
1½ tsp ground cumin
1 tsp salt
½ tsp pepper
¼ tsp ground cinnamon
1 egg
10 g/¼ oz fresh breadcrumbs
4 pittas and lemon wedges, to serve

yogurt mint sauce
10 g/¼ oz fresh mint leaves
280 g/10 oz natural yogurt
juice of ½ lemon
½ tsp salt
¼ tsp cayenne pepper

salad
1 cucumber, diced
2 tbsp chopped fresh flat-leaf parsley
140 g/5 oz cherry tomatoes, halved
juice of 1 lemon
½ tsp salt

1. Preheat the oven to 190°C/375°F/Gas Mark 5 and spray a large baking sheet with oil. Put the lamb, onion, garlic, cumin, salt, pepper, cinnamon, egg and breadcrumbs into a large bowl, mix well to combine and shape into 2.5-cm/1-inch balls.

2. Place the meatballs on the prepared baking sheet and spray with oil. Bake in the preheated oven for about 15 minutes, until cooked through.

3. Meanwhile, wrap the pittas in foil and put them in the oven. To make the sauce, finely chop the mint. Put the mint into a small bowl with the remaining ingredients and stir well.

4. To make the salad, put the cucumber, parsley and tomatoes into a medium-sized bowl and mix to combine. Add the lemon juice and salt and stir to combine.

5. Remove the meatballs and bread from the oven. Cut the pittas in half. Stuff a few meatballs into each half and spoon in some of the sauce. Serve two halves per person with the salad and lemon wedges alongside.

cals: 595   fat: 31.7g   sat fat: 13.6g   fibre: 3g   carbs: 47.1g   sugar: 7.3g   salt: 4.1g   protein: 30g

prawn rice paper rolls

prep: 40-45 mins
cook: no cooking

40 g/1½ oz rice vermicelli noodles

150 g/5½ oz chilled cooked tiger prawns, rinsed with cold water, drained and sliced

grated zest of 1 lime

10 g/¼ oz fresh mint leaves, torn from stems

10 g/¼ oz fresh coriander, long stems trimmed

55 g/2 oz beansprouts, rinsed and drained

55 g/2 oz carrots, cut into matchstick strips

¼ cucumber, halved lengthways, deseeded and cut into matchstick strips

½ cos lettuce heart, leaves shredded

12 x 20-cm/8-inch rice spring roll wrappers

dipping sauce

juice of 1 lime

1 tbsp tamari

1 tbsp light muscovado sugar

1 tsp Thai fish sauce

1 red chilli, halved, deseeded and finely chopped

2 garlic cloves, finely chopped

2.5-cm/1-inch piece fresh ginger, scrubbed and finely grated

1. Add the noodles to a shallow dish, cover with just boiled water, then leave to soften for 5 minutes. Mix the prawns with the lime zest. Arrange the mint, coriander, beansprouts, carrot sticks, cucumber sticks and shredded lettuce in separate piles on a tray. Drain the noodles and tip into a dish.

2. Pour some just boiled water into a large, shallow round dish then dip one of the rice wrappers into the water. Keep moving in the water for 10–15 seconds until soft and transparent, then lift out, draining well, and place on a chopping board.

3. Arrange a few prawn slices in a horizontal line in the centre of the rice wrapper, leaving a border of wrapper at either end. Top with some mint leaves and coriander sprigs, then add a few noodles and beansprouts. Add some carrot and cucumber and a little lettuce. Roll up the bottom third of the rice wrapper over the filling, fold in the sides, then roll up tightly to form a sausage shape. Place on a separate tray.

4. Repeat with the remaining wrappers until you have 12 rolls. To make the dip, add the lime juice to a small bowl, stir in the tamari, sugar and fish sauce, then add the chopped chilli, garlic and ginger, and stir.

5. Cut each roll in half and serve immediately with individual bowls of the dipping sauce. If planning to serve later, wrap each roll in clingfilm, pour the dipping sauce into a small container and chill in the refrigerator for up to 8 hours.

top tip

Don't be tempted to overfill the rice wrappers or they will be too difficult to roll.

reduced
calorie

makes 12

cals: 68   fat: 0.6g   sat fat: 0.1g   fibre: 1.2g   carbs: 12g   sugar: 2.3g   salt: 0.6g   protein: 3.8g

salmon croquettes

prep: 35 mins, plus chilling
cook: 40 mins

300 g/10½ oz floury potatoes, peeled
  and halved

300 g/10½ oz cooked salmon, flaked

8 tbsp chopped fresh dill,
  plus extra to garnish

6 spring onions, some green parts
  included, finely chopped

1 tbsp cornflour, sifted

1 tsp salt

½ tsp pepper

2 eggs, lightly beaten

flour, for dusting

oil, for frying

aioli

3 large garlic cloves

1 tsp sea salt flakes

2 egg yolks, at room temperature

250 ml/9 fl oz extra virgin olive oil

2 tbsp lemon juice

1. Bring a large saucepan of water to the boil,
add the potatoes, bring back to the boil and
cook for 20 minutes, or until tender. Drain
well, mash and set aside.

2. Put the salmon, potato, dill and spring
onions into a large bowl and lightly mix with
a fork. Sprinkle with the cornflour, salt and
pepper. Stir in the eggs.

3. With floured hands, form the mixture into
eight patties about 2 cm/¾ inch thick. Place
on a baking sheet lined with baking paper and
chill for at least 2 hours.

4. To make the aioli, use a mortar and pestle
to crush the garlic and salt to a smooth paste.
Transfer to a large bowl. Beat in the egg yolks.

5. Add the oil, a few drops at a time, whisking
constantly, until thick. Beat in the lemon juice.
Cover with clingfilm and set aside.

6. Heat the oil in a frying pan and cook the
croquettes over a medium–high heat for 8
minutes, until golden. Turn and cook the other
side for 4–5 minutes, until golden. Garnish
with dill and serve immediately with the aioli.

reduced sugar

cals: 487   fat: 45.6g   sat fat: 7g   fibre: 1.3g   carbs: 9.5g   sugar: 0.9g   salt: 1.6g   protein: 11g

fish patties with olive tartare sauce

prep: 45 mins, plus chilling
cook: 55-60 mins

500 g/1 lb 2 oz baking potatoes,
  cut into chunks

500 g/1 lb 2 oz boneless firm white fish
  fillets, such as hake, pollack or haddock

25 g/1 oz unsalted butter

finely grated zest and juice of
  1 unwaxed lemon

4 tbsp milk

25 g/1 oz fresh flat-leaf parsley,
  finely chopped

40 g/1½ oz fresh chives, finely snipped

1 egg

4 slices of wholemeal bread, processed in
  a food processor to make crumbs

40 g/1½ oz Parmesan cheese,
  finely grated

1 tbsp virgin olive oil

salt and pepper

85 g/3 oz mixed green salad leaves,
  to serve

lemon wedges, to serve (optional)

olive tartare sauce

70 g/2½ oz herb-marinated green and
  black olives, stoned and chopped

150 g/5½ oz natural yogurt

1. Half-fill the base of a steamer with water, bring to the boil, then add the potatoes to the water and cook for 15 minutes. Put the fish in the steamer top in a single layer, cover with a lid and steam for 8–10 minutes, or until it flakes easily when pressed with a knife and the potatoes are tender.

2. Drain the potatoes, add the butter, lemon zest and juice and 2 tablespoons of milk, and mash together. Remove any skin from the fish, flake the flesh into bite-sized pieces, then add it to the mash with 15 g/½ oz each of the parsley and chives and a little salt and pepper, then fold everything together carefully. Divide the mixture into eight portions, then shape each into a thick round and leave to cool.

3. Crack the egg into a shallow bowl, add the remaining 2 tablespoons of milk and beat with a fork. Put the breadcrumbs, remaining parsley, 15 g/½ oz chives and the Parmesan on a plate and mix together. Coat each fish patty in the egg, then dip it into the crumb mixture to coat completely. Chill in the refrigerator for 30 minutes.

4. Preheat the oven to 200°C/400°F/Gas Mark 6. Brush a large baking sheet with a little oil, add the fish patties, then drizzle with a little extra oil. Bake for 25–30 minutes, turning halfway through cooking, until browned and piping hot.

5. Meanwhile, make the olive tartare sauce. Put the olives, yogurt, remaining chives and a little salt and pepper in a bowl, and mix well. Serve the fish patties with spoonfuls of the sauce, the green salad leaves and lemon wedges, if using, for squeezing over.

fact

Fish is a great source of lean protein and essential fatty acids, which protect against heart and circulation problems.

High protein

serves 4

cals: 445 fat: 16.9g sat fat: 7.3g fibre: 6g carbs: 38g sugar: 6.2g salt: 3.6g protein: 34.5g

snack time

Whether you get pre-lunch stomach rumbles or a 4pm sugar-dip, sometimes you just need a snack. All too often, though., these are highly processed with very little nutritional value. This chapter shows you how to make healthy snacks that will keep you going in between meals.

time saving

Nearly all of the recipes in this chapter can be made in advance to save time, then carried around with you or kept in the refrigerator to have on hand for whenever the munchies strike! They're also great for taking to work or packing into school lunchboxes.

snack attack

smoky paprika roasted chickpeas

prep: 15–20 mins, plus cooling
cook: 18–24 mins

2 tbsp olive oil

1 tsp cumin seeds, roughly crushed

1 tsp smoked paprika

¼ tsp ground allspice

¼ tsp ground cinnamon

½ tsp sea salt flakes

800 g/1 lb 12 oz canned chickpeas in water, drained

2 tbsp date syrup

1. Preheat the oven to 200°C/400°F/Gas Mark 6. Add the oil to a roasting tin and place in the oven to heat for 3–4 minutes. Mix together the cumin seeds, paprika, allspice, cinnamon and salt in a small bowl.

2. Add the chickpeas to the oil, drizzle over the date syrup, sprinkle with the spice mix and stir well. Roast in the preheated oven for 15–20 minutes, stirring once, until brown and crusty.

3. Spoon into a bowl and leave to cool before eating. Store any leftovers in a plastic container or spring-clip preserving jar in the refrigerator for up to 12 hours.

reduced
sat fat

top tip

Spices contain high levels of
antioxidants, which are essential
for fighting disease – and they're
easily added to many dishes.

cals: 227   fat: 9g   sat fat: 1.2g   fibre: 4g   carbs: 26.2g   sugar: 2.9g   salt: 0.7g   protein: 9.1g

fruit, nut & seed trail mix

200 g/7 oz unblanched almonds

25 g/1 oz pine nuts

25 g/1 oz pumpkin seeds

25 g/1 oz sunflower seeds

25 g/1 oz dried banana chips

55 g/2 oz dates, stoned and
roughly chopped

2 tbsp oat bran

½ tsp ground mixed spice

1 small egg white

1. Preheat the oven to 200°C/400°F/ Gas Mark 6. Put the almonds, pine nuts, pumpkin and sunflower seeds, banana chips, dates, oat bran and mixed spice in a large bowl and mix well.

2. Lightly beat the egg white with a fork. Add to the nut mixture, stirring to coat all the ingredients evenly.

3. Spread the mixture out on a large baking sheet in a single layer. Bake for 8–10 minutes, or until crisp and lightly browned. Leave to cool completely. Serve or pack into an airtight container and eat within five days.

3

top tip

For a savoury mix, replace the bananas and dates with 85 g/3 oz cashew nuts, and the mixed spice with 1 teaspoon of mild curry powder and a large pinch of sea salt.

High
fibre

cals: 314   fat: 23.9g   sat fat: 2g   fibre: 6.3g   carbs: 20.7g   sugar: 8.6g   salt: trace   protein: 11.2g

asian spiced edamame & cranberries

prep: 15 mins, plus cooling
cook: 15 mins

350 g/12 oz frozen edamame (green soya) beans

5-cm/2-inch piece fresh ginger, peeled and finely grated

1 tsp Sichuan peppercorns, roughly crushed

1 tbsp soy sauce

1 tbsp olive oil

3 small star anise

40 g/1½ oz dried cranberries

1. Preheat the oven to 180°C/350°F/Gas Mark 4. Place the beans in a roasting tin, then sprinkle over the ginger and peppercorns. Drizzle with soy sauce and oil, and mix together.

2. Tuck the star anise in among the beans, then roast, uncovered, in the preheated oven, for 15 minutes.

3. Stir in the cranberries and leave to cool. Spoon into a small jar and eat within 12 hours.

High
protein

top tip

Edamame beans are extremely versatile and pack a much greater nutritional punch than frozen peas.

cals: 183   fat: 9.1g   sat fat: 1g   fibre: 4.3g   carbs: 12.8g   sugar: 7.4g   salt: 0.6g   protein: 11.4g

broad bean hummus
with crudités

prep: 30-35 mins
cook: 15 mins

350 g/12 oz podded broad beans

2 tbsp virgin olive oil

1 tsp cumin seeds, crushed

3 spring onions, thinly sliced

2 garlic cloves, finely chopped

25 g/1 oz fresh mint, torn into pieces

25 g/1 oz fresh flat-leaf parsley,
   finely chopped

juice of 1 lemon

60 g/2¼ oz Greek-style natural yogurt

salt and pepper

to serve

1 red and 1 yellow pepper, deseeded
   and cut into strips

4 celery sticks, cut into strips

½ cucumber, halved, deseeded and
   cut into strips

1 pitta, cut into
   strips (optional)

1. Half-fill the base of a steamer with water, bring to the boil, then put the beans in the steamer top. Cover and steam for 10 minutes, or until tender. Meanwhile, heat the oil in a frying pan over a medium heat. Add the cumin, spring onions and garlic, and cook for 2 minutes, or until the onion has softened.

2. Put the beans in a food processor, add the onion mixture, herbs, lemon juice and yogurt, and season with a little salt and pepper. Process to a coarse purée, then spoon into a dish set on a large plate. Arrange the vegetable strips around the hummus and serve with the pittas, if using.

top tip

As a rough guide you will need to buy about 750 g/1 lb 10 oz broad beans in their pods to get about 350 g/12 oz when podded.

cals: 206   fat: 8.6g   sat fat: 1.5g   fibre: 9g   carbs: 20.3g   sugar: 6.4g   salt: 1.6g   protein: 10.3g

goat's cheese truffles with honey

prep: 15 mins, plus chilling
cook: no cooking

reduced sugar

150 g/5½ oz French rindless soft goat's cheese

1 tsp clear honey

40 g/1½ oz pistachio nuts, finely chopped

salt and pepper

1. Mix the cheese and honey with a little salt and pepper in a bowl.

2. Scoop heaped teaspoons of the mixture onto a plate to make about 12 mounds.

3. Scatter the nuts over a separate, smaller plate, then roll one mound of cheese at a time in the nuts until evenly coated and shaped like a ball.

4. Place on a plate and chill in the refrigerator for 1 hour before serving. Pack any leftover truffles into a small plastic container and store in the refrigerator for up to 3 days.

variation

You could also roll small quantities of the truffles in different coatings — try chopped herbs or finely crushed pink peppercorns.

cals: 54   fat: 4.1g   sat fat: 2g   fibre: 0.3g   carbs: 1.5g   sugar: 0.8g   salt: 0.4g   protein: 3g

flavoured quinoa balls

prep: 35 mins, plus chilling
cook: 40 mins

115 g/4 oz quinoa

350 ml/12 fl oz boiling water

3 tomatoes, halved

2 garlic cloves, finely chopped

2 tsp torn fresh thyme leaves

2 tbsp virgin olive oil

115 g/4 oz young spinach leaves,
  rinsed and drained

175 g/6 oz feta cheese, drained weight,
  finely grated

pinch of grated nutmeg

25 g/1 oz stoned black olives,
  finely chopped

1 tbsp chopped fresh basil

salt and pepper

top tip

Ideal for work or school lunchbox
snacks, these balls of goodness can
be made in bulk and in advance.

1. Add the quinoa and water to a medium-sized saucepan, cover and cook over a medium heat for about 20 minutes, stirring occasionally, until the quinoa is soft and has absorbed all the water.

2. Meanwhile, preheat the grill. Arrange the tomatoes, cut-side up, on the base of a foil-lined grill rack. Sprinkle with the garlic, thyme and a little salt and pepper, then drizzle with 1 tablespoon of the oil and grill for 10 minutes.

3. Add the spinach to a dry, non-stick frying pan and cook for 2–3 minutes, until just wilted. Scoop the spinach out of the pan and finely chop, then mix with one third of the quinoa, one third of the cheese, a little nutmeg, and salt and pepper to taste.

4. Peel the tomatoes, chop and add with any pan juices to the empty spinach pan. Stir in half the remaining quinoa and cook for 2–3 minutes, until the mixture is dry enough to shape into a ball. Remove from the heat and stir in half the remaining cheese.

5. Mix the remaining quinoa and cheese with the olives, basil and a little salt and pepper. Shape each of the flavoured quinoa mixtures into eight small balls. Chill until ready to serve.

6. Preheat the oven to 180°C/350°F/Gas Mark 4. Brush a roasting tin with the remaining oil, add the quinoa balls and bake for about 10 minutes, turning once, until the edges are crisp and golden brown, and the cheese has melted. Serve hot.

reduced
sugar

makes 24

cals: 53   fat: 3.1g   sat fat: 1.3g   fibre: 0.6g   carbs: 4.3g   sugar: 0.8g   salt: 0.3g   protein: 2g

chicken & cheese-stuffed peppers

prep: 30-35 mins
cook: 15 mins

olive oil, for oiling

70 g/2½ oz full-fat cream cheese

2 garlic cloves, finely chopped

2 tsp finely chopped fresh rosemary

1 tbsp finely chopped fresh basil

1 tbsp finely chopped fresh parsley

15 g/½ oz finely grated Parmesan cheese

150 g/5½ oz cooked chicken breast, finely chopped

3 spring onions, finely chopped

12 mixed coloured baby peppers, about 350 g/12 oz total weight

salt and pepper

1. Preheat the oven to 190°C/375°F/Gas Mark 5. Lightly brush a large baking sheet with oil.

2. Put the cream cheese, garlic, rosemary, basil and parsley in a bowl, then add the Parmesan cheese and stir. Mix in the chicken and spring onions, then season.

3. Slit each pepper from the tip up to the stalk, leaving the stalk in place, then scoop out the seeds using a teaspoon.

4. Fill each pepper with some of the chicken mixture, then place on the prepared baking sheet. Cook in the preheated oven for 15 minutes, or until the peppers are soft and light brown in patches. Transfer to a plate to serve warm or cold.

reduced calorie

variation

You can stuff these sweet little peppers with any soft cheese, such as goat's cheese or ricotta.

cals: 60   fat: 3.2g   sat fat: 1.5g   fibre: 0.7g   carbs: 2.5g   sugar: 1.4g   salt: 0.4g   protein: 5g

chicken, kale & chia seed bites

prep: 20-25 mins, plus cooling
cook: 21 mins

2 skinless, boneless chicken breasts, about 125 g/4½ oz each

1 garlic clove, finely chopped

55 g/2 oz kale, shredded

115 g/4 oz light cream cheese

grated zest of ½ lemon

2 tsp chia seeds

salt and pepper

1. Place the chicken breasts in the top of a steamer half-filled with boiling water. Sprinkle with the garlic, season with salt and pepper, cover with a lid and cook over a medium heat for 20 minutes, or until the juices run clear when a skewer is inserted into the thickest part of the meat.

2. Add the kale to the steamer and cook for 1 minute to soften it slightly.

3. Remove the steamer from the pan and leave to cool, then finely chop the chicken and kale.

4. Mix the cream cheese, lemon zest and chia seeds together, then stir in the chicken and kale. Taste and adjust the seasoning if needed.

5. Using two teaspoons, scoop spoonfuls of the mixture onto a plate, scraping off with the second spoon. Roll the mixture into balls, then pack into a plastic container. Seal and store in the refrigerator for up to 2 days.

top tip

This is a great way to use up the leftovers from a roast chicken that aren't quite enough to make into a supper. Begin the recipe at step 2 and add the cooked chicken to the cooled kale.

High
protein

cals: 36   fat: 1.6g   sat fat: 0.7g   fibre: 0.3g   carbs: 1.2g   sugar: 0.4g   salt: 0.3g   protein: 4.1g

turkey & rainbow chard roll-ups

prep: 30-35 mins, plus chilling
cook: no cooking

8 rainbow chard leaves and stems (choose leaves that are about the same size as the slices of turkey), cut into matchstick strips

8 thin slices cooked turkey

150 g/5½ oz hummus

2 spring onions, trimmed and cut into very fine strips

1 carrot, cut into matchstick strips

100 g/3½ oz courgettes, cut into matchstick strips

1 avocado, halved, stoned, peeled and thinly sliced

juice of 1 lemon

1. Separate the chard leaves and arrange shiny side down on a large chopping board. Cover each one with a slice of turkey, then spread the turkey with a little hummus.

2. Divide the chard stems, spring onions, carrot and courgettes between the chard leaves, making a little pile on each leaf that runs in the centre of the leaf from long edge to long edge.

3. Top the little mounds with the avocado slices and a little lemon juice, then roll up from the base of the leaf to the tip and put on a plate, join downwards. Continue until all the leaves have been rolled.

4. Cut each roll into thick slices and transfer to individual plates, or wrap each roll in clingfilm and chill for up to 1 hour.

reduced calorie

variation

For a higher-carb, pre-workout version of this dish, replace the chard with wholemeal tortillas.

cals: 104   fat: 6.1g   sat fat: 1g   fibre: 3.6g   carbs: 17.5g   sugar: 1.6g   salt: 0.5g   protein: 6.5g

making healthy swaps

To fuel our bodies effectively – without the rollercoaster of highs and lows – we need good-quality protein, healthy fats, some carbohydrates and lots of vegetables. However, choosing foods that are nutrient-dense isn't always easy. To make sure you're getting enough essential vitamins, minerals and antioxidants, it is usually better to prepare food yourself.

A slice of cake or takeaway might seem like a good choice when you're short of time, but they are full of empty calories, saturated fats and highly-processed sugars that will soon make your energy levels plummet. Even when preparing food at home, it's easy to slip into the trap of using similar processed ingredients. Before you start cooking, make sure your storecupboard is fully stocked with all the wholesome staples you will need to prepare tasty and nutritious meals.

swap this

for that!

White flour
...which has been processed to remove the bran (that contains all the good fibre) then often bleached with a whitening agent.

Wholemeal flour
...or if you prefer to use gluten-free flours, try buckwheat flour, almond flour, coconut flour or hemp flour.

White sugar
...which is raw cane sugar that has been processed then treated to remove the molasses.

Light or dark muscovado sugar
...or if you're following a low-sugar diet, try replacing your usual granulated sugar with stevia – a natural plant extract.

White bread
...which is made using white, refined flour that has been stripped of its nutritious fibre and which is rapidly absorbed by the body as sugar.

Wholegrain bread
...which still contains all the nutrient-rich bran and germ that are removed when making white flour. It is also lower in calories than its white counterpart.

White rice
...which has undergone a process to remove its nutritious outer hull, leaving the grain with a mere fraction of its original vitamins and minerals.

Wholegrain rice
...which is full of dietary fibre, magnesium and protein. It also has a much lower glycaemic rating, which helps to reduce insulin spikes and fat storage.

Golden syrup
...which has a nutritional profile virtually identical to white table sugar and, like sugar, contains no vitamins or minerals.

Honey
...or if you're trying to reduce the amount of sugar in your diet, try replacing with rice malt syrup – a fructose-free sweetener made from fermented cooked brown rice.

Milk chocolate
...which is much higher in carbohydrates (sugars) and in combination with its fat content can increase weight gain.

Plain chocolate
...chocolate with 70 per cent cocoa or more contains a lot less sugar and more beneficial cocoa butter than milk chocolate varieties.

rosemary, sea salt & sesame popcorn

prep: 10-15 mins
cook: 6-8 mins

40 g/1½ oz sesame seeds

2 tbsp olive oil

2 rosemary stems,
   torn into large pieces

200 g/7 oz popping corn

1 tsp sea salt flakes

2 tbsp balsamic vinegar, or to taste

1. Add the sesame seeds to a large frying pan with 1 teaspoon of the oil, cover and cook over a medium heat for 2–3 minutes, shaking the pan, until the seeds are golden brown and beginning to pop. Scoop out of the pan into a bowl and wipe out the pan with a piece of kitchen paper.

2. Add the remaining oil and the rosemary to the pan and gently heat, shaking to release the rosemary's oil. Add the corn, cover and cook over a medium heat for 3–4 minutes, shaking the pan, until all the popcorn has popped. Remove from the heat.

3. Sprinkle with the toasted sesame seeds and season with the salt and vinegar, then tip into a serving bowl, discarding the rosemary.

High fibre

top tip

Popcorn is a natural wholegrain, low in fat and a great source of energy-producing complex carbohydrates - much better than crisps!

cals: 379   fat: 25.2g   sat fat: 3.2g   fibre: 6.6g   carbs: 30g   sugar: 1.6g   salt: 1.5g   protein: 6.4g

root vegetable crisps with yogurt dip

prep: 30-35 mins, plus chilling
cook: 12-16 mins

1 kg/2 lb 4 oz mixed root vegetables, such as carrots, parsnips or sweet potatoes and golden beetroot, very thinly sliced

4 tbsp virgin olive oil

sea salt and pepper

yogurt dip

200 g/7 oz Greek-style natural yogurt

2 garlic cloves, finely chopped

4 tbsp finely chopped fresh herbs, such as flat-leaf parsley, chives, basil or oregano

1. Preheat the oven to 200°C/400°F/Gas Mark 6. To make the yogurt dip, spoon the yogurt into a bowl, then stir in the garlic and herbs, and season with salt and pepper. Cover and chill in the refrigerator.

2. Put the vegetables in a large bowl. Slowly drizzle over the oil, gently turning the vegetables as you go, until they are all coated.

3. Arrange the vegetables over three baking sheets in a single layer, then season with salt and pepper. Bake for 8–10 minutes then check – the slices in the corners of the trays will cook more quickly, so transfer any that are crisp and golden to a wire rack. ww

4. Cook the rest for 2–3 minutes more, then transfer any more cooked crisps to the wire rack. Cook the remaining slices for a further 2–3 minutes, if needed, then transfer to the wire rack and leave to cool.

5. Arrange the crisps in a large bowl and serve with the dip.

top tip

When thinly slicing root vegetables, you should ideally use a mandolin. If you don't have one, a very sharp small knife will do the trick.

reduced sugar

cals: 294   fat: 16.6g   sat fat: 3.7g   fibre: 8.5g   carbs: 30.8g   sugar: 15.8g   salt: 1.8g   protein: 7.9g

roasted kale crisps

prep: 20 mins
cook: 10-12 mins

250 g/9 oz kale, thick stems and
  central rib removed, leaves rinsed,
  dried and torn into bite-size pieces

2 tbsp olive oil

2 pinches of sugar

2 pinches of salt

2 tbsp toasted flaked almonds,
  to garnish

1. Preheat the oven to 150°C/300°F/Gas Mark
2. Place the kale in a bowl with the oil and
sugar, then toss well.

2. Spread about half the leaves in a single
layer in a large roasting tin, spaced well apart.
Sprinkle with salt and roast on the bottom
rack of the preheated oven for 4 minutes.

3. Stir the leaves, then turn the tray so the
back is at the front. Roast for a further 1–2
minutes, until the leaves are crisp and very
slightly browned at the edges. Repeat with the
remaining leaves and salt. Sprinkle the kale
crisps with the flaked almonds and serve.

top tip

Watch your kale very closely; if it
overcooks and the leaves turn brown
they will be bitter.

serves 4

reduced
sat fat

cals: 123   fat: 9.8g   sat fat: 1.1g   fibre: 1.8g   carbs: 7.8g   sugar: 0.8g   salt: 0.8g   protein: 3.1g

apple & cinnamon crisps

prep: 20–25 mins, plus cooling
cook: 1½–2 hours

1 litre/1¾ pints water
1 tbsp salt
3 dessert apples, such as
  Braeburn or Gala
pinch of ground cinnamon

1. Preheat the oven to 110°C/225°F/ Gas Mark ¼. Put the water and salt into a large mixing bowl and stir until the salt has dissolved.

2. Very thinly slice the apples with a sharp knife or mandolin, leaving the skin on and the core still in place, but removing any pips. Add each apple to the water when you finish slicing it. Turn to coat in the salt water, which will help prevent the apple slices discolouring during baking.

3. Drain the apple slices in a colander, then lightly pat dry with a clean tea towel. Arrange in a single layer on a large wire cooling rack or roasting rack. Place this in the oven so that the heat can circulate under the slices as well as over the tops.

4. Bake for 1½–2 hours, until the apple slices are dry and crisp. Loosen with a palette knife, then sprinkle with cinnamon. Leave to cool completely, then pack into a plastic container, seal with a lid and keep in the refrigerator for up to 2 days.

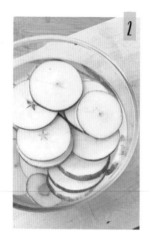

serves 4

top tip

If using a fan oven, put it on its lowest setting so that the apples dry out without colouring too much.

cals: 72   fat: 0.2g   sat fat: trace   fibre: 3.4g   carbs: 19.1g   sugar: 14.2g   salt: 0.7g   protein: 0.3g

fudge brownie
quinoa cookies

prep: 30 mins, plus cooling
cook: 12-14 mins

55 g/2 oz coconut oil

100 g/3½ oz plain chocolate,
   70% cocoa solids, broken into pieces

55 g/2 oz quinoa flour

1 tbsp cocoa powder

1 tsp bicarbonate of soda

½ tsp ground cinnamon

2 eggs

150 g/5½ oz light muscovado sugar

1 tsp natural vanilla extract

fact

Quinoa flour is a great alternative to wheat flour if you're gluten-intolerant, and the plain chocolate in these cookies adds richness — no one will ever guess they're healthy!

1. Preheat the oven to 190°C/375°F/Gas Mark 5. Line three baking sheets with baking paper.

2. Place the oil and chocolate in a bowl set over a saucepan of gently simmering water, making sure that the bowl is not touching the water. Heat for 5 minutes, or until the oil and chocolate have melted, then stir to mix. Remove from the heat and leave to cool slightly.

3. Add the quinoa, cocoa powder, bicarbonate of soda and cinnamon to a separate bowl and stir together.

4. Add the eggs, sugar and vanilla extract to a large mixing bowl and whisk together until thick and frothy. Gently fold in the oil and chocolate mixture, then add the flour mixture and stir until smooth.

5. Drop dessertspoons of the brownie mixture on the prepared trays, spaced well apart, then bake in the preheated oven for 7–9 minutes, until crusty and cracked and still slightly soft to the touch. Leave to cool and harden a little on the trays, then lift off the paper and pack into a biscuit tin. Eat within 3 days.

reduced calorie

cals: 78   fat: 4.3g   sat fat: 3g   fibre: 0.7g   carbs: 9.1g   sugar: 7.1g   salt: trace   protein: 1.2g

chocolate & peanut butter balls

prep: 20-25 mins, plus chilling
cook: no cooking

50 g/1¾ oz almond flour

60 g/2¼ oz unsweetened peanut butter

20 g/¾ oz unsalted peanuts,
   roughly chopped

3 tbsp linseeds

30 g/1 oz plain chocolate with
   85% cocoa solids, finely chopped

1 tsp cocoa powder

salt

1. Put the almond flour in a food processor and process for a minute, until you have the texture of rough flour. Put the peanut butter, peanuts, linseeds, chocolate and a pinch of salt in a bowl and mix. Add the almond flour, reserving 1½ tablespoons. Mix until you have a thick, chunky texture.

2. Sprinkle the remaining almond flour and cocoa powder onto a plate and mix with a teaspoon. Form a tablespoon of the peanut mixture into a ball using your palms. Roll in the cocoa powder mixture, then transfer to a plate. Repeat to make another seven balls. Cover and allow to chill in the refrigerator for at least 30 minutes before serving.

top tip

If the coating of cocoa powder is too bitter and strong for your taste, substitute it with half cocoa powder, half ground cinnamon.

makes 8

reduced sugar

cals: 139   fat: 11.5g   sat fat: 2.1g   fibre: 3g   carbs: 6.1g   sugar: 2g   salt: 0.1g   protein: 4.8g

wholemeal banana flatbread bites

reduced sat fat

prep: 15-20 mins
cook: 5-6 mins

4 x 20-cm/8-inch wholemeal
    tortilla wraps
4 tbsp tahini
3 tbsp date syrup
4 bananas

1. Preheat a dry frying pan, then add the tortillas, one by one, and warm for 30 seconds on each side.

2. Arrange the tortillas on a chopping board, thinly spread each with the tahini, then drizzle with the date syrup. Add a whole peeled banana to each tortilla, just a little off centre, then roll up tightly.

3. Cut into thick slices and arrange on a plate. Serve warm.

superfood chocolate bark

prep: 20-25 mins, plus setting
cook: 5 mins

100 g/3½ oz plain chocolate, 70% cocoa solids, broken into pieces

85 g/3 oz mixed Brazil nuts, unblanched almonds and pistachio nuts, roughly chopped

2 tbsp dried goji berries, roughly chopped

2 tbsp dried cranberries, roughly chopped

1 tbsp chia seeds

1. Place the chocolate in a bowl set over a saucepan of gently simmering water and heat for 5 minutes until melted.

2. Line a large baking sheet with baking paper. Stir the chocolate, then pour it onto the paper and spread to a 20 x 30-cm/8 x 12-inch rectangle.

3. Sprinkle the nuts, berries and seeds over the top, then leave to set in a cool place or the refrigerator. To serve, lift the chocolate off the paper and break into rough-shaped shards. Store in a plastic container in the refrigerator.

variation

This delicious chocolate bark is a blank canvas — try topping with any of your favourite superfoods, such as hemp seeds or medjool dates.

cals: 227   fat: 11.3g   sat fat: 2.5g   fibre: 4.1g   carbs: 60g   sugar: 25.4g   salt: 0.5g   protein: 9.4g

the main event

Preparing healthy and wholesome main meals is no more time-consuming than any other dish and the whole family will reap the benefits. A lot of the recipes in this chapter use sustaining, lean protein and vegetable combinations to ensure you get your quota of vitamins and minerals.

what's for dinner?

squash, kale & farro stew

prep: 20-25 mins
cook: 1 hour

2 tbsp vegetable oil

1 onion, finely chopped

2 tsp dried oregano

1 dense-fleshed squash, such as Kabocha or Crown Prince, weighing about 1.25 kg/2 lb 12 oz, peeled, deseeded and cut into quarters

2 garlic cloves, finely sliced

400 g/14 oz canned chopped tomatoes

750 ml/1¼ pints vegetable stock

125 g/4½ oz quick-cook farro, rinsed

250 g/9 oz kale, sliced into ribbons

400 g/14 oz canned chickpeas, drained and rinsed

6 tbsp chopped fresh coriander

juice of 1 lime

salt and pepper

1. Heat the oil in a flameproof casserole or heavy-based saucepan. Add the onion and fry over a medium heat for 5 minutes, until translucent. Add the oregano and garlic and fry for 2 minutes. Add the squash and cook, covered, for 10 minutes.

2. Add the tomatoes, stock and farro, cover and bring to the boil. Reduce the heat to a gentle simmer and cook for 20 minutes, stirring occasionally.

3. Add the kale and chickpeas. Cook for a further 15 minutes, or until the kale is just tender. Season to taste with salt and pepper. Stir in the coriander and lime juice just before serving.

reduced
calorie

top tip

Use quick-cook farro (farro dicocco)
so you can add it straight to the
casserole without lengthy soaking
or pre-cooking.

cals: 304   fat: 7g   sat fat: 1.1g   fibre: 8.9g   carbs: 55.6g   sugar: 10.2g   salt: 2.4g   protein: 10.3g

rice & lentil curry

cook: 20 mins

cook: 25–30 mins

2 tbsp olive oil

2.5-cm/1-inch piece fresh ginger, peeled and finely chopped

2 garlic cloves, finely chopped

1 onion, diced

2 tbsp curry powder

1 tsp salt

2 carrots, diced

225 g/8 oz cauliflower, chopped

225 g/8 oz kale, thick stems and centre ribs removed

90 g/3¼ oz basmati rice

90 g/3¼ oz small green lentils or red lentils

750 ml/1¼ pints vegetable stock or water

125 ml/4 fl oz coconut milk

juice of 1 lime

natural yogurt and sriracha sauce, to serve (optional)

1. Heat the oil in a large frying pan over a medium–high heat. Add the ginger, garlic and onion and cook, stirring, for about 2 minutes until the onion begins to soften. Stir in the curry powder and salt.

2. Add the carrots, cauliflower, kale, rice, lentils, stock and coconut milk, and bring to the boil.

3. Reduce the heat to low, cover and simmer for 15–20 minutes, until the lentils and rice are tender. Add the lime juice and stir. Serve immediately topped with yogurt and sriracha sauce, if using.

top tip

To save time, use washed and chopped ready-to-cook vegetables.

cals: 387   fat: 16g   sat fat: 7.8g   fibre: 12.6g   carbs: 53.7g   sugar: 6.9g   salt: 3.3g   protein: 12.6g

quinoa & beetroot burgers

prep: 30-35 mins, plus chilling
cook: 1¼ hours

3–4 small raw beetroot, about
   225 g/8 oz in total, peeled and cut
   into small cubes

135 g/4¾ oz quinoa, rinsed

350 ml/12 fl oz vegetable stock

½ small onion, grated

finely grated rind of ½ lemon

2 tsp cumin seeds

½ tsp salt

¼ tsp pepper

1 large egg white, lightly beaten

quinoa flour, for dusting

vegetable oil, for shallow-frying

slices of sourdough toast and peppery
   green salad leaves, to serve (optional)

wasabi butter

1½ tsp wasabi powder

¾ tsp warm water

70 g/2½ oz butter,
   at room temperature

1. Cook the beetroot in a steamer for 1 hour. Meanwhile, put the quinoa into a saucepan with the stock. Bring to the boil, then cover and simmer over a very low heat for 10 minutes. Remove from the heat, but leave the pan covered for a further 10 minutes to allow the grains to swell. Fluff up with a fork and spread out on a tray to dry.

2. To make the wasabi butter, mix together the wasabi powder and water. Mix with the butter and chill in the refrigerator.

3. Place the beetroot in a food processor and process until smooth. Tip into a bowl and mix with the quinoa, onion, lemon rind, cumin seeds, salt, pepper and egg white. Divide the mixture into eight equal-sized portions and shape into burgers, 15 mm/⅝ inch thick, firmly pressing the mixture together. Lightly dust with quinoa flour.

4. Heat a thin layer of oil in a non-stick frying pan. Add the burgers and fry over a medium–high heat, in batches if necessary, for 2 minutes on each side, turning carefully. Place the burgers on the toast, if using, and serve with the wasabi butter and salad leaves, if using.

makes 8

cals: 194   fat: 13.7g   sat fat: 5.3g   fibre: 2.3g   carbs: 15.1g   sugar: 2.4g   salt: 1g   protein: 3.6g

spinach, feta & tomato tart

prep: 35 mins, plus chilling
cook: 1 hour 5 mins–1¼ hours

15 g/½ oz unsalted butter

3 spring onions, thinly sliced

200 g/7 oz baby spinach

100 g/3½ oz fresh podded peas

3 eggs

250 ml/9 fl oz milk

100 g/3½ oz feta cheese,
    drained and finely crumbled

115 g/4 oz cherry tomatoes

salt and pepper

pastry

115 g/4 oz unsalted butter,
    cut into cubes

225 g/8 oz wholemeal plain flour,
    plus extra to dust

2 eggs, beaten

1. To make the pastry, put the butter and flour in a mixing bowl and season with salt and pepper. Rub the butter into the flour until it resembles fine crumbs. Gradually mix in enough egg to make a soft but not sticky dough.

2. Lightly dust a work surface with wholemeal flour. Knead the pastry gently, then roll it out on the work surface to a little larger than a 25-cm/10-inch loose-bottomed flan tin. Lift the pastry over the rolling pin, ease it into the tin and press it into the sides. Trim the pastry so that it stands a little above the top of the tin to allow for shrinkage, then prick the base with a fork. Cover the tart case with clingfilm and chill in the refrigerator for 15–30 minutes. Meanwhile, preheat the oven to 190°C/375°F/ Gas Mark 5.

3. To make the filling, melt the butter in a frying pan over a medium heat. Add the spring onions and cook for 2–3 minutes, or until softened. Add the spinach, turn the heat to high, and cook, stirring, until wilted. Set aside to cool.

4. Cook the peas in a saucepan of boiling water for 2 minutes. Drain, then plunge into iced water and drain again. Crack the eggs into a jug, add the milk, some salt and pepper, and beat.

5. Line the tart case with a large sheet of baking paper, add baking beans and place on a baking sheet. Bake for 10 minutes, then remove the paper and beans and bake for 5 minutes more, or until the base of the tart is crisp and dry.

6. Drain any cooking juices from the spring onions and spinach into the eggs. Put the onion mixture in the tart case, add the peas, then sprinkle over the cheese. Fork the eggs and milk together, then pour into the tart case and dot the tomatoes over the top. Bake for 40–50 minutes, or until set and golden. Leave to cool for 20 minutes, then serve.

High
protein

serves 6

cals: 447   fat: 28.1g   sat fat: 16g   fibre: 6.1g   carbs: 35.2g   sugar: 4.8g   salt: 1.7g   protein: 16.8g

chicken traybake

prep: 20-25 mins
cook: 50-60 mins

2 tbsp olive oil

4 chicken legs, about 350 g/12 oz each, left whole or cut into drumsticks and thighs

2 red peppers, deseeded and thickly sliced

1 large courgette, halved lengthways and thinly sliced

1 large onion, finely chopped

1 fennel bulb, thickly sliced lengthways

800 g/1 lb 12 oz canned chopped tomatoes

1 tbsp dried dill

1 tbsp balsamic vinegar

pinch of soft light brown sugar

salt and pepper

fresh crusty bread, to serve (optional)

1. Preheat the oven to 190°C/375°F/Gas Mark 5. Heat the oil in a frying pan. Add the chicken pieces, working in batches, if necessary, and fry for 5–7 minutes, until golden. Remove from the pan and keep hot.

2. Pour off all but 2 tablespoons of the oil. Add the red peppers, courgette, onion and fennel and fry, stirring, for 3–5 minutes, until the onion is soft. Stir in the tomatoes, dill, vinegar and sugar, and season with salt and pepper.

3. Place the chicken pieces on a baking tray and pour the vegetables over. Cover tightly with foil and bake in the preheated oven for 30–35 minutes, until the chicken is cooked and the juices run clear when a skewer is inserted into the thickest part of the meat. Serve with crusty bread, if using.

serves 4

fact

Mediterranean-style dishes like
this are hailed for their abundance
of vegetables and healthy fats.

cals: 467   fat: 23.3g   sat fat: 5.3g   fibre: 8.6g   carbs: 31.2g   sugar: 22g   salt: 2.4g   protein: 35.7g

chicken with pomegranate tabbouleh

225 g/8 oz wheatberries

4 raw beetroot (approx 350 g/12 oz), cut into cubes

500 g/1 lb 2 oz skinless, boneless chicken breasts, thinly sliced

1 small red onion, thinly sliced

200 g/7 oz cherry tomatoes, halved

seeds of 1 small pomegranate

2 tbsp roughly chopped fresh mint

70 g/2½ oz baby spinach

salt and pepper

dressing

juice of 1 lemon

4 tbsp virgin olive oil

2 garlic cloves, finely chopped

1 tsp light muscovado sugar

1. Half-fill the base of a steamer with water, bring to the boil, then add the wheatberries to the water. Put the beetroot in the steamer top, cover with a lid and steam for 20–25 minutes, or until the wheatberries and beetroot are cooked. Drain the wheatberries.

2. Meanwhile, to make the dressing, put the lemon juice, oil, garlic and sugar in a jam jar, season with salt and pepper, then screw on the lid and shake well.

3. Put the chicken in a bowl, add half the dressing and toss well. Preheat a griddle pan over a medium–high heat. Add the chicken and cook, turning once or twice, for 8–10 minutes, or until golden and cooked through. To make sure the chicken is cooked, cut into the middle and check there are no remaining traces of pink or red.

4. Put the red onion, tomatoes and pomegranate seeds in a large, shallow bowl. Add the wheatberries, beetroot and mint. Divide the spinach between four plates, spoon the wheatberry mixture over them, then arrange the chicken on top. Serve with the remaining dressing in a small jug.

chicken tagine with freekeh

prep: 30 mins
cook: 55-60 mins

1 tsp harissa paste

1 tbsp cumin seeds

½ tsp pepper

1 tsp salt

125 ml/4 fl oz olive oil

1 kg/2 lb 4 oz mixed root vegetables,
  such as carrots, turnips and potatoes,
  peeled and cut into large chunks

8 chicken thighs, about
  150 g/5½ oz each

2 onions, chopped

2 large garlic cloves, thinly sliced

150 ml/5 fl oz chicken stock

225 g/8 oz freekeh, rinsed

750 ml/1¼ pints water

6 tbsp chopped fresh coriander

1. Whisk together the harissa, cumin seeds, pepper, ½ teaspoon of the salt and 5 tablespoons of the oil. Pour half over the root vegetables and toss to coat. Rub the remainder into the chicken.

2. Heat 2 tablespoons of the remaining oil in a large flameproof casserole. Add the onions and fry gently for 5 minutes. Add the garlic and fry for a further 2 minutes. Add the vegetables, cover and fry for a further 10 minutes.

3. Heat the remaining oil in a frying pan. Add the chicken and cook, turning, for 6–8 minutes, until brown all over, then add to the vegetable mixture. Pour in the stock, cover and simmer for 30 minutes, or until the chicken is cooked through. Meanwhile, put the freekeh into a saucepan with the water and the remaining salt. Bring to the boil, cover and simmer for 25 minutes.

4. Tip the chicken and vegetables into a colander set over a large bowl. Pour the drained juices back into the casserole and simmer for 5 minutes, until thickened. Drain the freekeh and tip into a large serving dish. Arrange the chicken and vegetables on top, pour over the juices and sprinkle with the coriander to serve.

cals: 1004   fat: 63.3g   sat fat: 13g   fibre: 15.8g   carbs: 70.2g   sugar: 14.5g   salt: 2.5g   protein: 46g

turkey & barley stew

prep: 20 mins
cook: 33–35 mins

15 g/½ oz dried ceps

2 tbsp olive oil

1 onion, diced

450 g/1 lb button mushrooms, sliced

4 carrots, sliced

1 tsp salt

½ tsp pepper

200 g/7 oz barley

600 ml/1 pint vegetable stock, chicken
    stock or water

1 tbsp fresh thyme leaves or rosemary
    leaves, finely chopped

450 g/1 lb turkey breast meat, cut into
    1-cm/½-inch cubes

55 g/2 oz freshly grated Parmesan
    cheese

2 tbsp chopped fresh flat-leaf parsley

1. Place the ceps in a small bowl and cover with hot water. Heat the oil in a large saucepan over a medium–high heat. Add the onion and cook, stirring frequently, for about 4 minutes, until soft. Add the button mushrooms and carrots to the pan with the salt and pepper. Cook, stirring occasionally, for a further 4 minutes, until the vegetables are tender. Add the barley and stir to mix well. Add the stock.

2. Remove the ceps from the soaking water, reserving the soaking liquid, and chop. Add to the pan with the soaking liquid and bring to the boil. Add the thyme, reduce the heat to low and simmer, uncovered, for about 5 minutes.

3. Add the turkey to the stew, stir to mix, and then cover and simmer for 15 minutes, until the turkey is cooked through, the barley is tender, and most of the liquid has evaporated. Serve the stew in bowls, garnished with the cheese and parsley.

serves 4

top tip

To add some greens, slice 225 g/
8 oz of kale into ribbons and add to
the stew with the turkey breast

cals: 517   fat: 13.7g   sat fat: 4.4g   fibre: 13.8g   carbs: 58g   sugar: 9.4g   salt: 3.8g   protein: 44.2g

steak with spicy greens

prep: 20 mins
cook: 10-12 mins, plus resting

2 sirloin steaks, 280 g/10 oz each

2 tbsp olive oil

1 tbsp sesame oil

3 tbsp light soy sauce

2 tsp toasted sesame seeds

1 tsp pepper

2 garlic cloves

2-cm/¾-inch piece fresh ginger

1 small red chilli

2 spring onions

400 g/14 oz trimmed Asian greens
(such as kai-lan and pak choi)

1 tbsp sesame seeds

1. Season the steaks with 1 tablespoon of the olive oil, the sesame oil, 1 tablespoon of the soy sauce, the toasted sesame seeds and pepper. Preheat a large frying pan over a medium–high heat, add the steaks and cook for 3 minutes on each side for medium-rare. Rest for 5 minutes before serving.

2. Meanwhile, finely chop the garlic, ginger and chilli, and finely slice the spring onions. Return the pan to the heat and add the remaining olive oil, the garlic, ginger, chilli, spring onions and greens and stir-fry until the greens begin to wilt. Add the remaining soy sauce and the sesame seeds, and serve immediately with the sliced steak.

1

top tip

If you prefer steak medium, cook for about 4 minutes on each side. Remember to get the pan nice and hot before cooking the steak.

High
protein

what is a superfood?

'Superfoods' have been celebrated by nutritionists as being beneficial for health and wellbeing for years. These nutrient-dense foods offer a bundle of essential vitamins, minerals, protein and healthy fats – and many of these ingredients are more familiar to us than you might think.

Superfoods can be bought easily from supermarkets, farmers' markets and health shops and are often inexpensive, everyday ingredients. Thanks to their health-boosting qualities, they could almost be called 'natural medicines'.

10 superfoods you should be eating

Super greens
The deeper green vegetables are, the more lutein (an antioxidant related to vitamin A) they are likely to contain. Broccoli, cabbage, chard, kale, rocket and spinach are also rich in chlorophyll, which helps oxygenate the blood.

Red veg
Red beetroot and red peppers get their red pigment from the antioxidants betalains, which help protect against free-radical damage and provide a wide range of bioflavonoids, vitamins, minerals and carbohydrates.

Sunshine fruit and veg
Rich in beta-carotene, this bright-orange group contains carrots, pumpkins, butternut squash, sweet potatoes, papayas, mangoes and apricots.

Beta-carotene is important for boosting the immune system.

Fab fish
Salmon, trout, mackerel, fresh tuna and sardines are oily fish rich in protein, which is needed for the growth and maintenance of cells. They're also packed with Omega-3 essential fatty acids, which protect against heart and circulation problems.

Sustaining wholegrains

Rich in fibre, wholegrains leave you feeling fuller for longer and help to maintain a healthy digestive system and lower cholesterol. Opt for wholemeal flour for extra fibre, oats for a sustaining breakfast and quinoa instead of white rice.

Nuts and seeds

Packed with protein, nuts supply many of the same minerals that meat does, such as B vitamins, phosphorous, iron, copper and potassium. They are high in healthy fats and are one of the richest sources of vitamin E.

Amazing alliums

Garlic has been used for centuries to help fight infections, as it acts as an anti-microbial agent. Leeks also possess superfood properties, and are known for their useful amount of folate.

Energizing bananas

A banana is a terrific high-energy snack, and a great source of natural fruit sugars, starch and potassium to help regulate blood pressure and lower the risk of heart attacks and strokes.

Chocolate bliss

Provided you opt for varieties with 70 per cent cocoa solids or more, even chocolate can be beneficial to health. Packed with flavonoids that help reduce infection and protect cells, plain chocolate also contains the mineral magnesium, which is needed for nerve and muscle function.

Green tea

Long favoured by the Chinese for its health-giving properties, green tea contains an enhanced level of antioxidants and is known to have antibacterial and antiviral properties.

beef stew with kale & dumplings

prep: 40 mins
cook: 2 hours 40 mins-3 hours 20 mins

4 tbsp olive oil

½ onion, finely chopped

1 leek, thinly sliced

1 celery stick, roughly chopped

4 garlic cloves, finely chopped

1 level tsp tomato purée

900 g/2 lb beef shin, cut into bite-sized chunks

40 g/1½ oz quinoa flour

125 ml/4 fl oz brandy

800 ml/1 pint 7 fl oz beef stock

1 tbsp fresh thyme leaves

2 tbsp finely chopped flat-leaf parsley

2 tsp smoked paprika

6 cloves

2 fresh bay leaves

salt and pepper

200 g/7 oz kale, roughly chopped, to serve

juice of ¼ lemon, to serve

dumplings

125 g/4½ oz quinoa flour

20 g/¾ oz beef suet

60 g/2¼ oz Cheddar cheese, grated

1 tsp baking powder

1 tbsp fresh thyme leaves

2 tbsp finely chopped flat-leaf parsley

4 tbsp water

1. Heat 2 tablespoons of the oil in a large lidded casserole over a medium heat. Add the onion, leek and celery, and fry for 5 minutes, or until softened. Add the garlic and tomato purée, stir well, then turn the heat down to medium–low and leave to simmer while you cook the meat.

2. Heat the remaining 2 tablespoons of the oil in a large, heavy-based frying pan over a high heat until smoking hot. Season the beef with salt and pepper, then add it to the pan in batches and cook for a few minutes, turning, until browned on all sides. Using a slotted spoon, transfer the first batch to a plate while you brown the rest of the meat. Toss the browned meat into the casserole, then stir in the quinoa flour.

3. Turn the heat down to medium–high. Deglaze the beef frying pan with the brandy, being careful as it can flame. Scrape all the meaty goodness off the bottom of the pan into the bubbling brandy with a wooden spoon, then tip into the casserole. Pour in the stock, then add the thyme, parsley, paprika, cloves and bay leaves, and season with salt and pepper.

4. Bring to the boil, then turn the heat down to low and put on the lid. Simmer for 2–2½ hours, or until the sauce is thick and the meat is soft enough to pull apart with a spoon.

5. To make the dumplings, put the quinoa flour, suet, cheese, baking powder, thyme and parsley in a large bowl and mix well. Add the water a little at a time, mixing, until you have a firm dough. Shape the mixture into 12 small balls.

6. After 2–2½ hours cooking, remove the lid from the stew and arrange the dumplings on top. Put the lid back on and cook for 20 minutes, or until cooked through. Cook the kale in a large pan of boiling water for 2 minutes. Drain, then squeeze over the lemon juice and toss. Serve with the stew.

top tip

When selecting leafy greens, the deeper the green the better as these vegetables are rich in iron.

High
protein

serves 4

cals: 796   fat: 35.9g   sat fat: 11.7g   fibre: 6.2g   carbs: 42.1g   sugar: 2.6g   salt: 3.8g   protein: 62.2g

black rice risotto with parma ham

prep: 20 mins
cook: 1 hour 10 mins

200 g/7 oz black rice

6 Parma ham slices

1 tbsp olive oil

2 small heads chicory, quartered lengthways

15 g/½ oz butter

2 garlic cloves, thinly sliced

1 small shallot, roughly chopped

500 ml/17 fl oz chicken stock

2 level tbsp mascarpone cheese

2 tbsp roughly chopped fresh flat-leaf parsley

sea salt

fact

Black rice is arguably even better for you than wholegrain rice, because the bran hull contains significantly higher amounts of vitamin E, which boosts the immune system.

1. Cook the rice in a large pan of lightly salted boiling water for 45 minutes, or until tender but slightly chewy.

2. Heat a deep frying pan over a medium–high heat. Add the Parma ham and dry-fry for 30 seconds on each side, or until crisp. Transfer to a plate.

3. Add the oil to the pan, then fry the chicory for 2 minutes on each side, or until darkly golden. Remove from the pan, wrap in kitchen foil to keep warm and set aside.

4. Reduce the heat to medium, then melt the butter in the pan. Add the garlic and shallot, and fry for 4 minutes, or until softened. Add the cooked and drained rice and stock, bring to a simmer, then cook gently for 5 minutes, or until two-thirds of the liquid has been absorbed. Stir in the mascarpone and parsley, then return the chicory to the pan and warm through.

5. Crumble the Parma ham into large shards. Serve the risotto heaped into four bowls with the crisp ham on top.

reduced calorie

pork meatballs in chilli broth

prep: 30 mins, plus chilling
cook: 30 mins

1.2 litres/2 pints chicken stock

¼–½ fresh red chilli, deseeded and very finely sliced

½ tsp palm sugar or soft light brown sugar

3 fresh thyme sprigs

2 lemon grass stalks, fibrous outer leaves removed, stems bashed with the flat of a knife

1 small head pak choi, stems cut into small squares, leaves sliced into ribbons

1 spring onion, green parts included, sliced diagonally

dash of soy sauce

salt and pepper

pork meatballs

225 g/8 oz fresh pork mince

1 shallot, grated

2-cm/¾-inch piece fresh ginger, crushed

1 garlic clove, crushed

finely grated zest and juice of ½ lime

6 tbsp groundnut oil

salt and pepper

1. Pour the stock into a medium-sized saucepan. Add the chilli, sugar, thyme, lemon grass, a good pinch of pepper, and salt to taste and bring to the boil. Reduce the heat and simmer gently for 10 minutes. Remove from the heat and leave to cool for about 30 minutes.

2. To make the meatballs, combine the pork, shallot, ginger, garlic, lime zest and juice, and season. Mix well with a fork. Line a plate with kitchen paper.

3. Divide the mixture into 16–20 walnut-sized balls. Place on the prepared plate and chill for 30 minutes.

4. Heat a large wok over a high heat. Add the oil and heat until very hot. Add the pork meatballs and fry for 5–6 minutes, until golden brown all over and cooked through. Drain on kitchen paper and keep warm.

5. Remove the thyme and lemon grass from the broth. Add the pak choi and spring onion. Bring to the boil then simmer for 2 minutes until the pak choi stalks are just tender. Season with soy sauce. Ladle the broth and vegetables over the meatballs in bowls and serve immediately.

reduced sat fat

cals: 227   fat: 18.6g   sat fat: 6.2g   fibre: 1.2g   carbs: 6.2g   sugar: 1.9g   salt: 3.6g   protein: 10.7g

seared salmon with
garden greens

High
fibre

prep: 25 mins
cook: 30 mins

500 g/1 lb 2 oz baby new potatoes, unpeeled, scrubbed and any larger ones halved

1 tbsp virgin olive oil

finely grated zest and juice of 1 unwaxed lemon

1 tsp set honey

1 tsp wholegrain mustard

4 wild salmon fillets, about 150 g/5½ oz each

250 g/9 oz runner beans, cut into thin slices

250 g/9 oz asparagus

175 g/6 oz baby peas in pods or sugar snap peas

1 fennel bulb, thinly sliced, green feathery tops torn into pieces

6 tbsp crème fraîche

salt and pepper

1. Half-fill the base of a steamer with water, bring to the boil, then add the potatoes to the water and cook for 15 minutes.

2. Preheat the grill to medium-high and line the grill pan with foil. Mix the oil, lemon zest and juice, honey and mustard together in a jug, then stir in a little salt and pepper. Arrange the salmon on the grill pan, spoon over the lemon mixture and grill, turning once, for 8–10 minutes, or until browned.

3. Put the beans in the steamer, set over the potatoes, cover with a lid and steam for the last 6 minutes. Add the asparagus and peas 3 minutes before the end of the cooking time. Add the sliced fennel 1 minute before the end of the cooking time.

4. Drain the potatoes, season with salt and pepper and roughly crush with a fork. Spoon into the centre of four plates. Mix the green vegetables with the crème fraîche and fennel tops, then spoon over the potatoes. Lay the salmon on top of the vegetables and spoon over the lemony pan juices. Serve immediately.

cals: 482   fat: 21.2g   sat fat: 7.4g   fibre: 9.3g   carbs: 37.3g   sugar: 8.5g   salt: 1.7g   protein: 36g

mediterranean sole

prep: 20 mins
cook: 20 mins

2 tbsp olive oil

1 shallot, chopped

1 garlic clove, finely chopped

1 fennel bulb, trimmed, cored and finely sliced

125 g/4½ oz couscous

240 g/8¾ oz drained canned, chopped tomatoes

350 ml/12 fl oz vegetable stock or water

35 g/1¼ oz stoned Kalamata olives, chopped

4 sole fillets, about 175 g/6 oz each

¼–½ tsp crushed chilli flakes

1 tbsp fresh oregano leaves or 1 tsp dried oregano

60 g/2¼ oz butter

50 ml/2 fl oz white wine

salt and pepper

1. Heat the oil in a large frying pan over a medium–high heat. Add the shallot, garlic and fennel and cook, stirring occasionally, for about 3 minutes, until the vegetables are soft. Stir in the couscous, tomatoes, stock, olives and 1 teaspoon of salt.

2. Lay the fish fillets on top of the couscous mixture in a single layer. Season with salt and pepper. Sprinkle the chilli flakes and oregano over the fish. Cut the butter into small pieces and scatter over the fish. Drizzle over the wine. Cover, reduce the heat to low, and cook for about 15 minutes, until the fish is cooked through. Serve immediately on warmed plates garnished with the fennel sprigs.

variation

Replace the sole with cod or halibut, or with peeled and deveined prawns. The beautifully flavoured couscous with olives and fennel would also work well with baked chicken.

serves 4

High protein

cals: 475   fat: 24.3g   sat fat: 9.9g   fibre: 5.3g   carbs: 4.8g   sugar: 4.8g   salt: 3.5g   protein: 27.9g

oven-baked fish & chips

reduced sat fat

prep: 25 mins
cook: 40 mins

675 g/1 lb 8 oz potatoes, scrubbed but not peeled, cut into 5-mm/¼-inch sticks

2 tbsp vegetable oil

675 g/1 lb 8 oz cod fillets, cut into strips

30 g/1 oz plain flour

2 large egg whites

200 g/7 oz panko breadcrumbs

vegetable oil cooking spray

salt and pepper

tartare sauce, to serve

salad

1 small cucumber

4–6 radishes

280 g/10 oz washed mixed baby salad leaves

1 lemon

1 tsp white wine vinegar

½ tsp salt

¼ tsp pepper

pinch of sugar

4 tbsp olive oil

1. Preheat the oven to 230°C/450°F/Gas Mark 8. Rinse the potato sticks with cold water, then pat dry with kitchen paper. Spread on a baking sheet in a single layer and toss with the vegetable oil. Season with ½ teaspoon of salt and bake in the preheated oven for 25 minutes.

2. Season the fish on both sides with ½ teaspoon of salt and ¼ teaspoon of pepper. Place the flour, egg whites and breadcrumbs in three separate shallow bowls. Beat the egg whites until frothy. Dip the strips in the flour, then in the egg, then roll in the breadcrumbs.

3. Remove the chips from the oven and push them to one side of the baking sheet. Arrange the fish on the other side in a single layer and spritz with the oil spray. Return to the oven and bake for 15 minutes, turning the fish once, until the fish is crisp and cooked through.

4. Meanwhile, make the salad. Slice the cucumber and radishes into a large salad bowl and toss with the salad leaves. Zest and juice the lemon and combine with the vinegar, salt, pepper and sugar in a small bowl. Whisk in the oil then toss with the salad. Serve the fish and chips with a dollop of tartare sauce and the salad on the side.

cals: 545   fat: 9.7g   sat fat: 1.2g   fibre: 5.2g   carbs: 77g   sugar: 2.9g   salt: 1.8g   protein: 42.1g

seafood bake

prep: 30 mins
cook: 30 mins

350 g/12 oz new potatoes, thinly sliced

4 fresh corn cobs, silks and husks removed

4 tbsp olive oil

1 tsp salt

60 g/2¼ oz butter, plus extra for greasing

juice of ½ lemon

3 garlic cloves, chopped

1 tbsp smoked paprika or sweet paprika

900 g/2 lb live small clams

900 g/2 lb live mussels

350 g/12 oz large raw prawns

125 ml/4 fl oz dry white wine

crusty bread, to serve (optional)

dipping sauce (optional)

115 g/4 oz butter

3 garlic cloves, finely chopped

1. Preheat the oven to 220°C/425°F/Gas Mark 7 and grease a large baking dish. Put the potatoes and corn into the prepared dish. Drizzle with half the oil and half the salt. Cover with foil and bake in the preheated oven for 20 minutes.

2. Meanwhile, melt the butter in a bowl in the microwave. Add the remaining oil, the lemon juice, garlic, paprika and remaining salt to the bowl, and stir to combine.

3. While the vegetables are still cooking, scrub the clams and scrub and debeard the mussels. Discard any clams or mussels with broken shells and any that refuse to close when tapped. Wash the prawns.

4. Remove the foil from the baking dish and add the clams and mussels, nestling them into the potatoes. Add the wine and replace the foil. Return to the oven for a further 5 minutes.

top tip

Try to select seafood that is as fresh as possible — buy from your local fishmonger.

5. Remove the foil from the baking dish and add the prawns in a layer on top. Drizzle the butter mixture over the seafood. Replace the foil and return the dish to the oven. Cook for a further 5 minutes, or until the prawns are pink and cooked through and the clams have opened (discard any clams or mussels that remain closed).

6. Meanwhile, make the dipping sauce, if using. Melt the butter in the microwave. Combine with the garlic in a small bowl. Serve the bake with small bowls of sauce and crusty bread for mopping up the juices, if using. Be sure to put out seafood forks, empty bowls for the shells and lots of serviettes.

High
protein

serves 4

cals: 593   fat: 31.3g   sat fat: 10.6g   fibre: 4.8g   carbs: 34.9g   sugar: 7.7g   salt: 3.9g   protein: 35.1g

have your cake and eat it

People might think that switching to a healthy diet means not having any treats, but you can still have your cake and eat it too by paying a little more attention to the ingredients you use. The recipes in this chapter are mostly low in sugar and processed foods, and use whole grains, dark chocolate and fresh fruit.

all things sweet

raw chocolate ice cream

prep: 15 mins, plus freezing
cook: no cooking

3 bananas, about 300 g/10½ oz, peeled
3 tbsp unsweetened cocoa powder
1 tbsp agave nectar

1. Cut the bananas into 2-cm/¾-inch pieces. Place them in a freezer bag and freeze for 3 hours.

2. Put the frozen bananas in a food processor or blender. Add the cocoa powder and agave nectar and process until smooth. Scoop and serve immediately or refreeze for a firmer consistency.

fact

Bananas are high-energy fruit that are particularly loaded with fibre and potassium. They are considered to be effective in lowering blood pressure.

reduced calorie

cals: 92   fat: 0.8g   sat fat: 0.4g   fibre: 3.3g   carbs: 23.2g   sugar: 12.8g   salt: trace   protein: 1.6g

raspberry & watermelon sorbet

prep: 30 mins, plus cooling & freezing
cook: 7–9 mins

115 g/4 oz golden caster sugar
150 ml/5 fl oz cold water
finely grated zest and juice of 1 lime
225 g/8 oz raspberries
1 small watermelon, deseeded, peeled and cut into chunks
1 egg white

variation

Experiment with different combinations of fruit in this recipe, such as strawberries and cantaloupe.

1. Put the sugar, water and lime zest in a small saucepan and cook over a low heat, stirring, until the sugar has dissolved. Increase to high until the mixture comes to the boil, then reduce the heat to medium and simmer for 3–4 minutes. Leave the syrup to cool completely.

2. Put the raspberries and watermelon in a food processor in batches and process to a purée, then press through a sieve into a bowl to remove any remaining seeds.

3. Tip the purée into a loaf tin, pour in the lime syrup through a sieve, then stir in the lime juice. Freeze for 3–4 hours, or until the sorbet is beginning to freeze around the edges and the centre is still mushy.

4. Transfer the sorbet to a food processor and process to break up the ice crystals. Put the egg white in a small bowl and lightly whisk with a fork until frothy, then mix it into the sorbet.

5. Pour the sorbet into a plastic or metal container, cover and freeze for 3–4 hours, or until firm. Allow to soften at room temperature for 10 minutes before serving.

High fibre

158

cals: 195   fat: 0.7g   sat fat: trace   fibre: 4.7g   carbs: 48.6g   sugar: 40.9g   salt: trace   protein: 2.6g

coconut rice pudding with pomegranate

prep: 20-25 mins, plus chilling
cook: 45-50 mins

55 g/2 oz pudding rice

200 ml/7 fl oz canned light coconut milk

200 ml/7 fl oz almond milk

25 g/1 oz golden caster sugar

1 cinnamon stick

2 gelatine leaves

1 pomegranate, separated into seeds

grated nutmeg, to sprinkle

4 tbsp pomegranate syrup, to serve (optional)

1. Combine the rice, coconut milk, almond milk, sugar and cinnamon in a saucepan over a high heat. Bring almost to the boil, stirring, then reduce the heat and cover. Simmer very gently, stirring occasionally, for 40–45 minutes, or until most of the liquid is absorbed.

2. Meanwhile, place the gelatine leaves in a bowl and cover with cold water. Leave to soak for 10 minutes to soften. Drain the leaves, squeezing out any excess moisture, then add to the hot rice mixture and stir lightly until completely dissolved. Spoon the rice mixture into four 150-ml/5-fl oz metal pudding basins, spreading evenly. Leave to cool, then cover and chill in the refrigerator until firm.

3. Run a small knife around the edge of each basin. Dip the bases briefly into a bowl of hot water, then turn out the puddings onto four serving plates.

4. Scatter the pomegranate seeds over the top, then sprinkle with grated nutmeg. Drizzle with a little pomegranate syrup, if using, and serve immediately.

reduced calorie

fact

A compound found only in pomegranates is shown to benefit the blood vessels and heart

baked passion fruit custards

prep: 20 mins, plus chilling
cook: 40-45 mins

2 passion fruit

4 large eggs

175 ml/6 fl oz coconut milk

3 tbsp artificial sweetener, such as
   stevia

1 tsp orange flower water

variation

Try replacing the passion fruit pulp on top
with another tropical fruit puree such as
mango or pineapple.

1. Preheat the oven to 180°C/350°F/Gas Mark 4. Halve the passion fruit, scoop out the flesh from three of the halves and push it through a sieve using the back of a spoon to remove the seeds.

2. Crack the eggs into a large bowl. Add the passion fruit juice, coconut milk, artificial sweetener and orange flower water, and whisk until smooth and airy.

3. Pour the passion fruit custard into four ramekins, place them in a roasting tin and pour in hot water to reach halfway up the dishes. Bake for 40–45 minutes, or until just set.

4. Scoop the pulp from the remaining passion fruit half and spoon a little onto each dish. Serve immediately, or cover with clingfilm and chill in the refrigerator for up to 8 hours.

chocolate & avocado puddings

prep: 20 mins, plus chilling
cook: 5 mins

55 g/2 oz plain chocolate, 70% cocoa solids, broken into pieces

1 large ripe avocado, halved and stoned

4 tbsp canned full-fat coconut milk

4 tsp maple syrup

½ tsp natural vanilla extract

pinch of salt

grated plain chocolate and lightly toasted coconut chips, to decorate (optional)

1. Place the chocolate in a heatproof bowl set over a saucepan of gently simmering water and heat for 5 minutes, making sure that the water doesn't touch the base of the bowl.

2. Scoop the avocado flesh from the skin into a food processor. Whizz until smooth, then add the coconut milk, maple syrup, vanilla extract and salt. Spoon in the melted chocolate and whizz until smooth.

3. Spoon the mixture into small shot glasses. Decorate the tops with a little grated chocolate and a few toasted coconut chips, if using. Serve immediately or chill in the refrigerator until needed.

High fibre

fact

Avocados are rich in healthy monounsaturated fat and are one of the most nutritionally complete fruits you can eat.

amaranth & berry desserts

prep: 15 mins, plus chilling
cook: 20 mins, plus standing

90 g/3¼ oz amaranth,
  soaked overnight

225 ml/8 fl oz water

350 g/12 oz frozen mixed berries, such
  as blackberries, blackcurrants and
  raspberries, thawed

6 tbsp sugar, or to taste

lemon juice, to taste

whipped cream, to serve (optional)

1. Drain the amaranth through a fine sieve, then put it into a saucepan with the water. Bring to the boil, then cover and simmer over a low heat for 15 minutes. Remove from the heat, but leave the pan covered for a further 10 minutes to allow the grains to swell.

2. Meanwhile, put the berries and sugar into a saucepan, heat over a medium heat until almost boiling, then reduce the heat to low and simmer for 3–4 minutes, until soft.

3. Set aside half the berries. Put the remainder into a blender and purée until smooth. Stir the purée into the amaranth with lemon juice to taste. Cover and chill in the refrigerator for 1 hour. Divide the mixture between four glasses or bowls. Stir in the reserved berries, top each with a spoonful of cream, if using, and serve immediately.

fact

One of the sacred foods of the Aztecs, amaranth is a pseudo-grain related to spinach. It is rich in protein and gluten-free.

reduced sat fat

cals: 200   fat: 1.6g   sat fat: 0.3g   fibre: 4.3g   carbs: 42.1g   sugar: 27.6g   salt: trace   protein: 3.9g

pineapple carpaccio
with mango sauce

prep: 20 mins
cook: no cooking

1 small pineapple
1 ripe mango
juice of ½ lime
115 g/4 oz natural yogurt

1. Trim the top and base from the pineapple, then cut off all the skin and remove the 'eyes'. Use a large, sharp knife to slice the pineapple into thin slices. Arrange the slices, overlapping, on a wide platter.

2. Peel, stone and chop the mango flesh, then sprinkle with lime juice and use a blender or food processor to process to a smooth purée.

3. Put the mango purée in a small bowl. Spoon in the yogurt and swirl to create a marbled effect.

4. Put the bowl of mango sauce in the centre of the platter. Serve the pineapple with the sauce spooned over the top.

1

variation

While fruit like pineapples and mangoes is high in natural sugars, it is a great alternative to a refined sugar-laden dessert!

reduced calorie

cals: 126   fat: 1.4g   sat fat: 0.7g   fibre: 2.9g   carbs: 29.2g   sugar: 24g   salt: trace   protein: 2.3g

chocolate soufflés

prep: 25 mins
cook: 23-26 mins

vegetable oil spray
25 g/1 oz unsalted butter
85 g/3 oz plain chocolate, 85% cocoa
  solids, finely chopped
175 ml/6 fl oz skimmed milk
25 g/1 oz cocoa powder
1 tbsp plain flour
1 tsp vanilla extract
pinch of salt
4 egg whites
110 g/3¾ oz caster sugar

fact

Good quality dark chocolate with 85% cocoa solids or more has been shown to have a multitude of health benefits, especially 'raw', unprocessed chocolate varieties.

1. Preheat the oven to 190°C/375°F/Gas Mark 5. Spray six x 175-ml/6-fl-oz ramekins with vegetable oil spray. Put the butter, chocolate and 4 tablespoons of the milk in a microwave-safe jug or bowl and microwave on high for 30 seconds. Stir until the chocolate is melted. Add the cocoa powder, flour, vanilla extract and salt, and beat until well mixed. Add the remaining milk and stir to combine.

2. In a large bowl, beat the egg whites with an electric hand-held mixer on high speed for about 3 minutes, or until stiff peaks form. Add the sugar, a little at a time, and continue to beat for about a further 2 minutes, or until the mixture is thick and glossy.

3. Gently fold a large dollop of the egg mixture into the chocolate mixture and stir to combine using a palette knife. Gently fold the chocolate mixture into the remaining egg mixture until well combined.

4. Carefully spoon the mixture into the prepared ramekins and bake in the preheated oven for about 22–25 minutes, or until the soufflés are puffy and dry on the top. Serve the soufflés immediately.

High
fibre

cals: 237   fat: 10.8g   sat fat: 6g   fibre: 3g   carbs: 30.8g   sugar: 23.5g   salt: 0.6g   protein: 5.6g

improve your health

A balanced and varied diet is crucial to your wellbeing, but other lifestyle choices can play important roles too. It is not only what you eat but also how much you eat that matters, as well as getting enough exercise into your daily routine. There are several tips you can use to help you achieve this balance.

Increase your exercise

Several worldwide studies have shown that many of us put on weight not because we are eating much more than we used to, but because we burn fewer calories through activity. We humans were designed to use our bodies – to walk, to run, to climb – but in the modern world it is easy to do very little. Cars, home appliances, the Internet, TV, office jobs, escalators and lifts all help to keep us sedentary.

Exercise not only helps keep your weight stable (and can actually help you lose weight), it has many other benefits too. It improves sleep patterns and insomnia, helps lift depression, keeps joints supple, improves posture, increases strength and mobility, improves heart and lung health and can even decrease the risk of diabetes.

Walking is ideal as it can be fitted in anywhere, is free and every minute counts as exercise. Try taking the stairs not the lift or walking one extra stop instead of taking the bus all the way. But also think about cycling, swimming or even dancing in your sitting room! Try to do at least 30 minutes a day, five days a week.

Make small changes

If you have been so busy that food has taken a backseat in your life, think about small ways you can make it more important. For example, try to take more time over buying, preparing and eating your food. Food is, or should be, a pleasure, not a chore – so use it as a way to be kind to yourself.

Get planning

Set aside 30 minutes or so at the weekend to plan some easy evening meal ideas, along with some healthy lunches to take to work and some nutritious breakfasts. Then, write your shopping list and enjoy a trip to the local shops or farmer's market to stock up. The results will almost always be healthier and tastier than those takeaways!

Keep tabs

When you buy ready-made foods, keep an eye on the labels so that you choose items that will fit in with your exercise levels, calorie and nutrition needs. Reduce your stress.

Watch your portions

Keep an eye on your portion sizes when you cook. It's tempting to make a little extra 'just in case' but only do that if you can make one and freeze one for another day. Cutting down portion sizes a little is a great way to lose weight and keep it off.

Eat regularly

It is better to eat small meals more frequently than to try to 'be good' and have just one big meal, for example. That often leads to bingeing and cravings, as well as making you feel dizzy or headachy. An ideal pattern is breakfast, lunch, a small late afternoon snack and an evening meal.

And...relax

Take time to relax and enjoy your food – chew everything well and really savour it. Research shows you eat less if you do this, rather than using a mealtime to work, read or watch TV.

raw date & nut bars

prep: 30 mins, plus chilling
cook: no cooking

400 g/14 oz medjool dates, halved and stoned

60 g/2¼ oz unblanched almonds

60 g/2¼ oz cashew nut pieces

35 g/1¼ oz chia seeds

2 tbsp maca

2 tsp natural vanilla extract

20 g/¾ oz desiccated coconut

55 g/2 oz unblanched hazelnuts, very roughly chopped

25 g/1 oz pecan nuts, broken in half

1. Add the dates, almonds and cashew pieces to a food processor and pulse until finely chopped. Add the chia seeds, maca and vanilla extract, and process until the mixture binds together in a rough ball.

2. Tear off two sheets of baking paper, put one on the work surface and sprinkle with half the coconut. Put the date ball on top then press into a roughly shaped rectangle with your fingertips. Cover with the second sheet of paper and roll out to a 30 x 20-cm/12 x 8-inch rectangle.

3. Lift off the top piece of paper, sprinkle with the remaining coconut, the hazelnuts and pecan nuts, then re-cover with the paper and briefly roll with a rolling pin to press the nuts into the date mixture.

4. Loosen the top paper, then transfer the date mixture, still on the base paper, to a tray and chill for 3 hours or overnight until firm.

5. Remove the top paper, cut the date mixture into 12 pieces, peel off the base paper then pack into a plastic container, interweaving the layers with pieces of baking paper to keep them separate.

goji, mango & pistachio chocolate slice

prep: 25 mins, plus chilling
cook: 6-8 mins, plus standing

1 tbsp light olive oil

40 g/1½ oz popping corn

115 g/4 oz crunchy peanut butter

2 tbsp coconut oil

2 tbsp maple syrup

6 tbsp full-fat milk

100 g/3½ oz plain chocolate, 85% cocoa solids, broken into pieces

25 g/1 oz dried goji berries, roughly chopped

25 g/1 oz dried mango slices, finely chopped

25 g/1 oz pistachio nuts, roughly chopped

15 g/½ oz sunflower seeds

15 g/½ oz pumpkin seeds

1. Line the base and sides of a 20-cm/8-inch shallow square cake tin with a sheet of baking paper.

2. Heat the olive oil in a frying pan, then add the corn, cover with a lid and cook over a medium heat for 3–4 minutes, until all the corn has popped. Transfer to a bowl, discarding any grains that haven't popped, and wipe out the pan with kitchen paper.

3. Add the peanut butter, coconut oil, maple syrup and milk, and gently heat for 2–3 minutes, stirring until smooth. Remove from the heat, add the chocolate and set aside for 4–5 minutes, until the chocolate has melted.

4. Add the popcorn to the chocolate mix and lightly stir together. Tip into the prepared tin, press down flat with the back of a fork, then sprinkle with the goji berries, mango, nuts, sunflower seeds and pumpkin seeds. Press the topping into the soft chocolate mix, then chill in the refrigerator for 2 hours, until firmly set.

5. Lift the paper and chocolate mixture out of the tin, place on a chopping board, peel away and reserve the paper, then cut into 12 pieces. Pack into a plastic container, layering between pieces of the reserved paper. Cover and keep in the refrigerator for up to 4 days.

reduced sugar

chocolate & macadamia cupcakes

prep: 25-30 mins, plus cooling
cook: 20 mins

85 g/3 oz butter, at room temperature

85 g/3 oz crunchy peanut butter

85 g/3 oz light muscovado sugar

2 eggs, beaten

115 g/4 oz wholemeal flour

1 tsp baking powder

55 g/2 oz macadamia nuts, roughly chopped, plus 12 whole nuts to decorate (optional)

chocolate frosting

100 g/3½ oz plain chocolate, 70% cocoa solids, broken into pieces

25 g/1 oz butter, diced

25 g/1 oz light muscovado sugar

4 tbsp milk

top tip

Choose ingredients that are as unrefined as possible. Opt for wholemeal flour instead of white flour and unrefined muscovado sugar instead of white sugar.

1. Preheat the oven to 180°C/350°F/ Gas Mark 4. Line a 12-hole muffin tin with paper cases. Add the butter, peanut butter and sugar to a large bowl and beat together until fluffy. Gradually beat in a little of the egg, alternating with a few spoonfuls of the flour, then continue until all the egg and flour have been added. Beat in the baking powder and chopped nuts.

2. Divide the mixture between the cases, bake in the preheated oven for 15 minutes until risen and golden brown. Leave to cool in the tins for 10 minutes. To make the frosting, put the chocolate, butter, sugar and milk into a heatproof bowl set over a saucepan of simmering water and heat, stirring occasionally, for about 5 minutes, until glossy.

3. Spoon the frosting over the cakes, then top each with a macadamia nut, if using. Leave to cool for 30 minutes. Remove from the tin.

High
fibre

cals: 274   fat: 19.2g   sat fat: 8.3g   fibre: 3g   carbs: 22.3g   sugar: 12.3g   salt: 0.5g   protein: 5.4g

gingered nut & oat cookies

prep: 25 mins, plus chilling
cook: 12-15 mins

175 g/6 oz unsalted butter, softened and diced, plus extra to grease

115 g/4 oz dark muscovado sugar

2.5-cm/1-inch piece fresh ginger, peeled and finely chopped

150 g/5½ oz wholemeal plain flour

85 g/3 oz porridge oats

70 g/2½ oz unblanched hazelnuts, roughly chopped

70 g/2½ oz unblanched almonds, roughly chopped

1. Place a sheet of baking paper about 30 cm/12 inches long on a work surface. Cream the butter, sugar and ginger together in a large bowl. Gradually beat in the flour, then the oats and nuts, until you have a soft dough. Spoon the mixture into a 25-cm/10-inch line along the baking paper, then press it into a 5-cm/2-inch diameter roll. Wrap in the paper and chill in the refrigerator for 30 minutes, or up to three days.

2. Preheat the oven to 180°C/350°F/Gas Mark 4. Grease two baking sheets with butter. Unwrap the cookie dough and slice off as many cookies as you require. Arrange on the baking sheets, leaving a little space between each. Bake for 12–15 minutes, or until cracked and browned at the edges. Leave the cookies to cool for 5 minutes, then loosen and transfer them to a wire rack to cool completely.

variation

Try these cookies with roughly chopped plain chocolate or dates and finely grated orange zest instead of the ginger and chopped nuts.

High protein

almond milk-and-cookie shots

High fibre

prep: 35 mins, plus chilling
cook: 18–20 mins

6 tbsp coconut oil, at room temperature, plus extra for oiling

55 g/2 oz light muscovado sugar

½ tsp natural vanilla extract

25 g/1 oz ground hazelnuts

25 g/1 oz ground golden linseeds

115 g/4 oz plain wholemeal flour

1 egg yolk

100 g/3½ oz plain chocolate, 70% cocoa solids

150 ml/5 fl oz unsweetened almond milk

1. Lightly grease 6 x 90-ml/3-fl oz dariole moulds and line with baking paper.

2. Beat together the oil, sugar and vanilla extract in a mixing bowl until creamy. Add the hazelnuts and linseeds, then add the flour and egg yolk, and beat together. Finely chop 30 g/1 oz of the chocolate and mix into the hazelnut mixture. Squeeze the dough into clumps. Divide between the moulds and, using a teaspoon, spread the mixture over the base and up the sides of the moulds to make cups.

3. Transfer to a baking tray and chill in the refrigerator for 20 minutes. Meanwhile, preheat the oven to 180°C/350°F/Gas Mark 4. Bake the cups in the preheated oven for 13–15 minutes, until golden brown, then reshape the inside of the cups with a teaspoon if the mixture has spread inwards. Leave to cool for 30 minutes.

4. Loosen the edges of the cups with a small knife and remove from the tin. They are very crumbly at this stage. Return to the tray and chill for at least 1 hour, until firmly set.

5. Break the remaining chocolate into a heatproof bowl set over a saucepan of gently simmering water and heat until melted. Add spoonfuls of melted chocolate to the cookie cases, then tilt and rotate the cases to cover the insides with chocolate. Chill for 30 minutes. When ready to serve, pour in the milk and serve as shots.

makes 6

cals: 573   fat: 39.7g   sat fat: 24.8g   fibre: 8.2g   carbs: 50.2g   sugar: 21.4g   salt: trace   protein: 8.6g

spicy squash cake

prep: 30 mins, plus soaking
cook: 1¼ hours

50 g/1¾ oz sultanas

450 g/1 lb butternut squash, peeled, deseeded and diced (prepared weight)

150 g/5½ oz unsalted butter, plus extra for greasing

150 g/5½ oz caster sugar

50 g/1¾ oz almonds, chopped

50 g/1¾ oz Italian mixed peel

finely grated rind of 1 lemon

1½ tsp ground cinnamon

1½ tsp ground ginger

85 g/3 oz khorasan flour

1 heaped tsp baking powder

2 eggs, separated

icing sugar, for dusting

fact

Khorasan is an ancient variety of Egyptian wheat. It is higher in protein than regular wheat and can be used in soups, stews, side dishes or even in baking!

1. Put the sultanas in a bowl, pour over boiling water to cover and leave to soak. Preheat the oven to 180°C/350°F/Gas Mark 4. Grease and line a 23-cm/9-inch springform cake tin.

2. Put the squash and butter into a saucepan. Cover and cook over a medium heat for 15 minutes, until soft. Tip into a bowl and beat until smooth. Stir in the sugar, almonds, mixed peel, lemon rind, cinnamon, ginger and sultanas, and mix well.

3. Sift together the flour and baking powder, tipping in any bran from the sieve. Gradually beat into the squash mixture. Beat the egg yolks for 3 minutes, until thick. Fold into the squash mixture.

4. Whisk the egg whites until they hold stiff peaks. Fold into the mixture using a metal spoon. Tip the batter into the prepared tin. Bake in the preheated oven for 1 hour, or until a skewer inserted into the centre comes out clean. Turn out onto a wire rack to cool. Dust with icing sugar just before serving.

High
fibre

cals: 384   fat: 21.2g   sat fat: 11g   fibre: 4.6g   carbs: 46.1g   sugar: 28.1g   salt: 0.4g   protein: 5.5g

clementine almond cake

prep: 35 mins, plus cooling
cook: 35-45 mins

125 g/4½ oz unsalted butter, plus extra
  for greasing

125 g/4½ oz caster sugar

4 eggs, separated

150 g/5½ oz millet flour

2 tsp gluten-free baking powder

125 g/4½ oz ground almonds

finely grated rind and juice of
  2 clementines

syrup

juice of 4 clementines

100 g/3½ oz caster sugar

topping

225 g/8 oz vegetarian low-fat soft curd
  cheese or quark

2 tbsp caster sugar

2 tbsp extra-thick double cream

1. Preheat the oven to 180°C/350°F/Gas Mark
4. Grease a 23-cm/9-inch springform cake tin.

2. Beat together the butter and sugar until
fluffy. Gradually beat in the egg yolks.
Combine the flour, baking powder and ground
almonds, then beat into the butter, sugar and
egg yolk mixture. Mix in the clementine juice,
reserving the rind.

3. Whisk the egg whites until they hold stiff
peaks. Fold into the mixture using a metal
spoon. Tip the batter into the prepared
tin. Bake in the preheated oven for 30–40
minutes, until a skewer inserted in the centre
comes out clean.

4. Meanwhile, to make the syrup, put the
clementine juice and sugar into a small
saucepan and boil for 3 minutes, until syrupy.
Make holes in the surface of the cake with a
skewer. Pour over the hot syrup. When it has
trickled into the holes, remove from the tin
and transfer to a wire rack to cool completely.

5. To make the topping, beat together the
curd cheese, sugar and cream. Spread over
the cake and sprinkle with the reserved
clementine rind.

High
protein

cals: 499   fat: 27.2g   sat fat: 11.4g   fibre: 2.5g   carbs: 53.5g   sugar: 37.1g   salt: 0.5g   protein: 12.5g

sweet potato brownies

prep: 25 mins, plus cooling
cook: 20 mins

150 ml/5 fl oz olive oil, plus extra to grease

175 g/6 oz sweet potatoes, coarsely grated

100 g/3½ oz artificial sweetener, such as stevia

50 g/1¾ oz cocoa powder

½ tsp baking powder

½ tsp bicarbonate of soda

50 g/1¾ oz ground almonds

2 eggs, beaten

20 g/¾ oz walnuts, roughly chopped

1. Preheat the oven to 180°C/350°F/ Gas Mark 4. Lightly oil a shallow 19-cm/ 7½-inch square cake tin, then line the base and sides with a large square of baking paper.

2. Put all the ingredients in a large bowl and stir well. Pour the mixture into the prepared tin. Bake for 20 minutes, or until well risen and the centre is only just set.

3. Leave to cool in the tin for 15 minutes. Lift out of the tin using the baking paper, then carefully remove the paper. Cut into 12 brownies to serve.

top tip

If this recipe is too chocolatey for your taste, reduce the amount of cocoa to 35 g/1¼ oz or serve with a dollop of crème fraîche.

reduced sugar

rhubarb & lemon
drizzle squares

reduced sat fat

prep: 30-35 mins, plus soaking
cook: 35-40 mins

300 g/10½ oz trimmed young rhubarb,
  cut into 2-cm/¾-inch thick slices

100 g/3½ oz ground almonds

115 g/4 oz brown rice flour

1½ tsp baking powder

1 ripe banana, mashed

150 ml/5 fl oz rice bran oil

115 g/4 oz light muscovado sugar

grated zest of 1 lemon

3 eggs

25 g/1 oz unblanched almonds,
  roughly chopped

syrup

juice of 2 lemons

60 g/2¼ oz light muscovado sugar

1. Preheat the oven to 180°C/350°F/Gas
Mark 4. Line the base and sides of a 30 x 20
x 4-cm/12 x 8 x 1½-inch rectangular cake tin
with baking paper.

2. Place the rhubarb in a dry roasting tin and
bake in the preheated oven for 10 minutes,
until almost soft. Remove from the oven but
do not switch the oven off. Put the ground
almonds, flour and baking powder into a bowl
and stir together.

3. Put the banana, oil, sugar and lemon zest
into a separate bowl and whisk together until
smooth. Whisk in the eggs, one at a time, then
beat in the flour mixture.

4. Spoon the batter into the prepared tin,
then scatter over the rhubarb. Bake for 25–30
minutes, until the cake is risen and the sponge
springs back when pressed with a fingertip.

5. To make the syrup, mix the lemon juice
with the sugar. Spoon half over the hot cake
and leave to soak in for 1–2 minutes. Spoon
over the remaining syrup, scatter with the
chopped almonds and leave to cool in the tin.
Lift the cake out of the tin, peel away the
paper and cut into 24 small pieces.

makes 9

cals: 400   fat: 26.1g   sat fat: 4.5g   fibre: 3.2g   carbs: 37.7g   sugar: 22.6g   salt: 0.3g   protein: 6.8g

index